C000057704

Where did our love go?

Where did our love go?

Reviving a marriage in 12 months

Yvonne Roberts

SHORT
BOOKS

First published in 2006 by
Short Books
15 Highbury Terrace
London N5 1UP

10 9 8 7 6 5 4 3 2 1

A CIP catalogue record for this book
is available from the British Library.

ISBN 1-904977-42-1

Printed in Great Britain by William Clowes Ltd, Beccles, Suffolk

Many thanks to Gillian Walton, Penny Mansfield, Ingrid, Tom and Dan. A thankyou, too, to Irene Boston who transcribed some of the interviews

We live in an age, in the so called "developed" world, in which love appears to be in short supply. It is rationed, withdrawn, denied; it is abused and corrupted, yet sought after; and it is treasured and much admired when it manifests itself in couples who are living happily ever after.

If surveys and polls are to be believed, the ideal of a monogamous, reasonably content, long-term union – inside or outside the church – is the goal of many. When the American writer Joan Didion wrote *The Year of Magical Thinking*, a moving articulation of grief at the death of her husband, John Gregory Dunne, she was surprised at the response. Her book tours attracted not the similarly bereaved, but 20 and 30 somethings. They were less concerned with how she handled her loss than interested in how she and Dunne had made a success of a forty-year marriage in which they had lived and worked together producing numerous screenplays.

"A lot of people seem to be reading the book for the relationship between me and my husband, " she told one inter-viewer. "They seem to be reading it as a marriage manual. I realised that was probably why it was being read so widely.".

Today, paradoxically, we have a mania for personal growth and revelation. Self-examination has become an art form yet when it comes to living in harmony with another human being in a long-term relationship, many of us have little idea how to make it flourish. We are experiencing what the American clinical psychologist Michael Vincent Miller calls "the contemporary crisis in intimacy".

In spite of a multi-million-pound self-help industry, today's couples still don't knwo how to deal with sex, power and vulnerability, let alone the practicalities of who does what, when and why. Instead, loving becomes yet another set of battle moves embracing neurosis, mind games and domes-tic guerilla warfare.

How do we balance autonomy and interdependence? How do we ease that eternal push and pull – the fear of abandonment versus the terror of becoming trapped and emotionally engulfed? Liz Hoggard, author of *How To Be Happy*, a book that examines the latest research into the new science of happiness, suggests having one hour of totally uninterrupted conversation with your partner every week. Small wonder that relationships rapidly become malnour-ished when forced to exist on a diet of so little time.

In previous centuries, relationships were more hard-head-ed affairs. They were dictated by survival or property or politics, or all three. Love was incidental. Now, fragile and delusional, love is all that counts. But working against its survival is a culture built of short-termism that regards an insatiable appetite for the latest and newest as proof of cutting edge coolness.

Advertising, minute by minute, pumps out propaganda which says in a market place of infinite variety that only the sad, lost and devout, choose to be "tied down". Yet, in a secular society, falling in love also offers the last chance of salvation. In the competitive, success obsessed society in which we live the natural rhythm of romance – give and take – is too often replaced by the ethos of the jungle: winning becomes more impotent than wooing.

Still, many of us continue to be old-fashioned romantics. We believe that the act of falling in love, that brief encounter with overwhelming emotions, adolescent in its single-minded intensity, should somehow be sufficient to weather disappointment, loss and years of familiarity. Years in which the irritating habits and imperfections of a spouse loom ever-larger, as the memory of what first attracted us so passionately is almost erased.

That initial adolescent idealisation of passion – call it fate, chemistry, biology, magic – that brings two people together is never enough for the long haul. Instead, as the relationship grows more toxic, the understanding that underpins it evaporates. Instead, we turn to blame. "Look, what you've done to me...." "I was never like this before I met you...." "I've given you the best years of my life – for what?"

How then do we forge a relationship that offers both security and autonomy, pleasure and joy, respect, humour and companionship? A relationship that allows each person to change and grow, both together and independently, one that provides fun and an erotic charge – unique to those who know each other well – and the capacity to surprise and delight? Is it worth the effort? Why bother when singles are allegedly having so much fun?

***

Ingrid and Tom have been together for ten years, and married for seven. They say they love each other – but for the past five years, for much of the time, they have been at war. Arguments, tension, silences and mutually bitter recriminations, perhaps familiar to many couples, now deeply scar their relationship.

But, now and again, there are fleeting moments when they are reminded of why they were first attracted to each other. They hope the damage can be mended – but they no longer know how.

The couple want to revive their relationship both for themselves and for the sake of their six-year-old son, Dan. He is bright, happy and appears well-adjusted. He is doing well at school, but the anger and distress and recurring threats of departure made by both parents have corroded his sense of security.

Like the vast majority of people in troubled relationships, Ingrid and Tom say counselling holds no appeal. An increasing number of couples choose to walk away from such relationships. According to surveys, many subsequently express regret that they did not try harder to resolve their problems.

But Tom an Ingrid did not walk away. In a last-ditch attempt to save their marriage, they answered an advertisement in a newspaper. The ad, placed in both the *Times* and the London *Evening Standard*, read, "Marriage under stress? Writer seeks a couple for a book. Married five years or more, with children, willing to discuss relationship on a regular basis and have access to expert advice – to see if relationship can be improved over a twelve-month period. Anonymity is possible."

This book is the story of what happened next.

CHAPTER ONE
Ingrid and Tom

In total, seventeen couples responded to the ads or were suggested by word of mouth. I chose Tom, then 35, and Ingrid, five years older han her husband, because they were both committed to the idea of sticking with the experiment for twelve months. They were both articulate, had rejected the idea of counselling earlier in their marriage, and came from very different backgrounds.

In the past, when society was less mobile, potential partners were often literally found on your door step; the boy or girl next door. That proximity could give a relationship a strong start – values; family; religion (or lack of it); upbringing would often be very similar reducing the opportunities for cultural clashes and misunderstandings. Now, we are much more cosmopolitan.

Tom and Ingrid also reflected the enormous social change that has occurred over the past forty or so years – in particular, the increase in women in the workplace and the rise in

12

divorce and families headed by a lone parent.

Tom had recently taken redundancy from a blue collar job in which he had been employed for eighteen years. He was at home, waiting to set up his own property business, having acquired several estate agent qualifications. He had the financial backing of a millionaire entrepreneur.

Tom is one of three children. He comes from a traditional working class family. Both his siblings are white collar professionals. Tom's mother does everything in the house and, according to Tom, "lives for her family". Tom's father, when Tom was growing up, would go to the pub several evenings a week. Tom had a volatile relationship with his dad as a teenager, but they grew closer in his thirties. Tom's sister, in her twenties and "very independent", is a business woman, She has multiple sclerosis and is married and lives in South Africa.

Ingrid is Scandinavian and worked in the fashion industry after leaving school, travelling abroad extensively. She came to London to attend a language course in 1995, aged 29, and met Tom, then 25, in a club. They married in 1997 when Ingrid was four months pregnant with their son.

When Ingrid was five her parents divorced. She was brought up by her mother and rarely saw her father. The household consisted of her mother, sister, aunts and two grandmothers. Ingrid's mother, a nurse, never remarried. Both Tom and Ingrid said they had happy childhoods.

Ingrid and Tom said that they were both committed to staying with each other – but, at our first meeting, it became plain that they had very different ideas of what "being married" actually involved on a day-to-day basis.

Tom felt his first duty was to act as breadwinner and put money on the table. Ingrid believed that "being together" wasn't just a matter of proximity, it also meant sharing a physical and emotional life that required Tom to spend less time at work or in the pub or watching football, and more time with her and their son. This conflict is a theme in many relationships.

As they spoke, often in competition with each other, I was drawn to both of them. They were both personable and easy to like, and seemed at ease with me. They made an attractive couple. Tom,was tall and dark with an open face and strong features, quick to smile. Ingrid was also tall and dark-haired, slim, dressed with style, again quick to find humour.

Over the year, I sometimes felt like banging their heads together because they were so adept at turning the tools of recovery into weapons to further emotionally disembowel each other. But I never stopped liking them. I did become emotionally involved. At different stages, I thought but didn't say, that Ingrid might be better off alone – or that Tom should give himself a break and move into a flat. Gradually, however, guided by expert advice, putting the clues together as in a detective story, I began to see what kept Ingrid and Tom together. To see what might persuade them to suspend hostilities and, as Tom put it, "learn to love each other again" proved more of a challenge.

Tom and Ingrid live in a rented flat in West London, close to Tom's family. Dan is charming and extrovert. They both said they hoped that the constant rows were not having an impact on him. "We tell him all the time that we love him and because mummy and daddy argue sometimes it's not his fault."

Ingrid and Tom share a sense of humour which, at our first meeting, served to mask some, but not all, of the tension. For the past three years, Ingrid has worked full-time as an events organiser in a Scandinavian company in London. Tom had been at home for two months prior to our first meeting waiting for his new business to begin. This had added to their difficulties because Ingrid wasn't used to her husband in the flat so much, and she felt that he did little to help domestically. Tom, in turn, believed that he helped a great deal with Dan. He said his wife was obsessively tidy and he could do nothing right. Again, common themes in relationships in which both partners work.

They agreed that I would interview them separately on a monthly basis. The transcripts of the interviews would be read by two experts: Gillian Walton, the former director of clinical and educational psychology at *Relationship Counselling for London,* and a respected counsellor with over 30 years experience; and Penny Mansfield, a family researcher, sociologist and writer, and director of the independent organisation, *One Plus One.* The latter conducts groundbreaking research on how relationships work and tests innovative ways of strengthening partnerships.

I had interviewed Penny frequently in the past for a range of articles on relationships, family break up and its impact on children. I'd found her open-minded, intuitive and well informed. She also had a strong belief in the capacity of couples to sort themselves out – according to Penny, "There is a natural genius in people to regenerate relationships. To some extent what we read in the media about the condition of partnership and marriage is unrepresentative. We hear a lot about people getting divorced or going to counsellors because that is what people talk about. What we know less about his how people sort things out in private, which is what they do most of the time."

Penny's research aims at understanding how and what makes marriages and cohabitations work, often against the odds. She has the rare gift of being able to translate complex social change into easily understood language that still carries both poetry and a punch. She also has a terrific sense of humour and an infectious passion for examining the ways in which we live together.

I had met Gillian a few years before when I interviewed her for an article. She exudes serenity and calm and thoughtfulness. Like Penny, Gillian also has a natural way with words, a strong sense of humour and a deep understanding. Importantly, her advice seemed rooted in the real world.

Interviewing her for an article on long-term monogamy the sharp increase in divorce in the 50-plus age group, she had said, "Perhaps we're beginning to see the swing of the pendulum. Perhaps we are growing more aware that to be truly intimate, you can't expect to walk only in the sunlight. You have to engage with the dark side of a relationship, too, and there are rewards in staying together. Couples have to keep changing, keep communicating and don't forget the erotic. People in their mid-50s are children of the 1960s.

They have a different attitude to sex. They are not going to give up as previous generations have done."

Every time we met, Gillian's comments literally made me feel as if a light had been switched on, illuminating what had previously been a very dark corner. Over the coming months, listening to both Gillian and Penny struggling not just to analyse what was wrong, but find ways to revitalise Ingrid and Tom's relationship, the same thought came to my mind: "So that's what it's really about..."

Each month, we met to unpick the possible sources of Tom and Ingrid's conflict and discuss ways to encourage change – suggestions which the couple could obviously accept or reject if they chose. Tom and Ingrid would be sent their own report each month but have no direct contact with Gillian or Penny.

Our goal: to take a forensic look at one relationship in crisis over a twelve-month period. We would offer neither therapy nor counselling, but insight and guidance from outsiders, at least two of whom had expertise in the psychology of relationships. We hoped the process might illuminate not just Tom and Ingrid's specific problems but also explain why so many of us are making a mess of the business of living happily ever after.

Gillian, Penny and I had to trust the other. And, in a sense, Gillian and Penny had to invest far more faith in the project than I did since journalism is, too often, based on betrayal and deception.

Since Ingrid and Tom were averse to counselling but willing to give regular interviews, Gillian and Penny had to rely on my ability to ask appropriate questions. I had to forego journalistic tactics, and be empathetic to both Tom and Ingrid without taking sides. Above all, I had to avoid collusion. No "How could he/she do that...?", however strong the desire – otherwise I risked becoming part of their marital problems. So, minus my usual tools, how was I going to persuade them to "open up"?

Gillian and Penny also warned that, on occasions, I would inevitably be exposed to two versions of the "truth" and implicitly asked by each partner to judge who was "right". If one partner was especially manipulative, or controlling, or skilled at making his or her own case, again, it might be difficult to avoid becoming entangled in the dynamics of the relationship.

We agreed that each partner would be interviewed separately and their interview would be confidential to them – although they could read the joint report. This was to avoid the interviews becoming "a right to reply" instead of exploring the relationship itself. The reports and edited interviews would make up part of the book.

We knew we would face ethical dilemmas which might not have easy solutions – for example, how much comment should we feed back each month? We had promised confidentialit, but what if one partner disclosed an affair? What if one partner physically assaulted the other ? We decided to deal with each crisis if and when it arose.

As it transpired, Gillian and Penny constantly offered wise counsel over the twelve months. Nothing in love is quite what it seems but they appeared to understand better than most what was concealed beneath the surface.

The five of us agreed the rules of engagement, a contract that was re-affirmed halfway through the year. One condition was that any of us could end the experiment at any time. We agreed that anonymity was vital both to encourage frankness and to protect Dan. It also ensured that the couple's motivation was to save their marriagerather than occupy the spotlight – however low the wattage.

Not one of us could predict the outcome. Tom and Ingrid might separate after three months, or turn a positive corner half way through the year, making the experiment redundant. Or they might tell us to clear off and mind our own business when the going got rough before the relationship improved. If it improved.

***

Our aim was to encourage Ingrid and Tom to believe that change – with all its risk and uncertainties – was better than remaining together mired in misery. By the end of the book, Ingrid and Tom will have spoken for themselves about the plusses and minuses of the exercise. For myself, I learned more over the course of that baffling year than I had in a lifetime about the mysterious ways in which grown-ups behave. I also discovered how little we really know about love.

Chapter Two

September – Tom: first interview

Our first meeting took place in a deserted hotel bar in central London. The first few questions felt odd: too restrained for an interview but also far too clumsy to encourage Tom to "open up" as he might to a counsellor.

"What don't you like about Ingrid?" would have been my preferred opener – but that would only have confirmed for Tom that many of the matrimonial problems were all Ingrid's fault.

My first challenge was to encourage them both to look at their own behaviour so I chose a suitably open-ended question.

***

Are you leading parallel lives at present?
Ingrid always says, "Are you going out? Are you going out now?" I'm not going nowhere but I'm not going to sit there

and have her shout at me... Ingrid will shout from the other end of the house – whereas I would come and speak, she shouts right across the house.

What does Dan do when she does that?

He just ignores it. He's really good at school. He socialises. He's open about everything. I tell him, "Dan, it's not about you. You've done nothing wrong. Mummy and Daddy are just being silly. We love you so much." We both reassure him. We go to great lengths to do that, both of us. I ask him, "What do you think about Mummy and Daddy shouting?" He says that sometimes he gets angry or he says, "I ignore you..."

I suppose as he gets older he'll...

Yeah, he'll resent us. It's not how families should behave.

Do you think your relationship is beyond repair?

Sometimes, I do think that. I think deep down Ingrid thinks the same. I don't think she knows if she loves me or not. I don't think I know if I love her or not. I think we are content in our own unhappiness, happy in our misery. *(Laughs)*

You're in a discomfort zone? But relationships can be turned around... If you did separate what would happen to Dan?

I suppose Ingrid would take him. I wouldn't just want to see him at weekends...

So, perhaps, that's an added incentive to stay together? Is the situation also affecting friends and family?

Family

Because?

I think they find Ingrid sort of difficult to get along with. Ingrid says, "Your mum knows something is wrong you know..." She makes faces to my mum (behind my back)... it's innuendo...

So why don't you let her speak about it to your mum?

I just don't let her. I don't mind if she wants to talk to my brother. We went out for dinner with them a couple of months ago. He had had an affair.

Does the wife know?

Yes. They seem okay. We ended up having a terrible row in the street. They said what's happening? What's going on? I felt it was Ingrid because she'd been drinking. She'll probably say it was my fault. Whatever, it doesn't matter. They didn't realise things were like that.

How long did he have an affair for?

Quite a long time, a couple of years maybe. Incredible really. They have two kids as well. I could accept a certain number of things because of Dan. If Ingrid was having an affair, it's probably because we're not together physically. I'd forgive certain things for Dan's sake. Who knows what people do in certain circumstances? I don't mind my brother and his wife involved but not my mum and dad.

When you thought about what married life might be like, did you assume it was going to be like your mum and dad's?

No – I had no preconceptions. I suppose I went into it, as I always do, thinking "Let's do it and we'll take it from there..." I suppose I live on my wits a little bit which is sometimes not a good thing to do.

It's very difficult. You must be feeling very unhappy?

Relationship wise, I'm just ticking along for Dan's sake. But obviously, I'd rather be happy. If this could work. I'm really prepared to give it a try. I don't believe it can work but that's not a fact, otherwise you wouldn't be here. I'm open to it. I really am. I'll take advice. I'll try to make things better. I'll put myself into it 100 per cent. If you tell me to do something. I'll do it properly.

How did you do at school?

I never liked school. I'm not one of those who looks back and says "best years of my life". No chance. I really hated it. I liked the people but I didn't enjoy the lessons. Which is not very good, is it? I didn't even get my results after I did my exams which is a terrible thing to say. I didn't do the homework. I got an O level in Biology because you had to do the least coursework. Terrible to say.

How did that compare with your brother and sister?

Brother left school with one O level; he went on to become quite well qualified. Sister got very good Os and As. She's quite an achiever. My sister's quite pushy, quite domineering. I think we are all quite strong personalities. Ingrid isn't submissive. We're not submissive in our attitude. The most compatible couples probably have one who is submissive.

Or perhaps they alternate...?

Mum and Dad have been married for 40-something years. Mum is the submissive one, she's a real housewife... she's really homely. She wouldn't go too far away. My dad would go round the world but she wouldn't go on holiday because of the grandchildren. Whereas my dad is a bit of a free spirit.

When you look at your mum and dad's relationship, would you say they've been happy?

Definitely. They very rarely... They might get flustered with each other but there's nothing serious ever. Mum's a giving person. You feel like you're taking something away if you're to do something [that she wants to do]...

Is she controlling?

No, not at all. She'll try and manipulate me in some ways. She'll say, "Bring some washing around". And I say, "Mum this isn't East Enders. We have got our own washing machine..."

(*Laughing*) Because they're always down the laundrette...?

They are really old-fashioned *(laughs)* – they wouldn't say, "Start your own business, take a gamble..." My dad, if a bill falls on the doormat, it's paid. They are great values really. I'm more likely, if I get parking tickets, to pretend they don't exist. They go in the drawer which is terrible really... I'm inconsistent about how I approach things like that... they only have one way.

You were 16, when you started work?

General dogsbody... 1986 or seven... I was doing an insurance job for a couple of months. My dad fixed me up. It was basically talking to people on the telephone about things they knew more about than me. It was terrible. No training sitting there with an old boy who had his coffee at the same second every day. It was a dull gloomy office, it was so not me. I took home £43 per week. I lasted a few weeks and I got the sack. I wasn't surprised. I was crap at it. I'm not a behind-the-desk person. [He gives details of his new company he's about to start – involving property.] I used to write poems and stuff. I used to have bad depressions when I was younger after bad times in a relationship I was in before. I lost my house at the same time and I almost got killed by the police.

God, three traumas at once... So what happened? You moved to work at the same place as your dad?

At that time, you had to be in the job for about twenty years before you become a manager. I had my feet up at work thinking, "someone take me away from all this..." The boss comes along. At the time, he was an Establishment figure, not like now. Old boy with a watch on a chain and all that... He stared at me. I thought I'm not going to put my feet down because you're looking at me. Next day, he asked "how do you fancy becoming a manager?" I was seventeen and no other manager is less than 40. I was a bit shocked.

What did you say?

I said no, but I was quite flattered. I think probably that was one of the turning points

Why say no?

I don't know what my friends would have said... I was young and stupid but then again, I'm pleased because I never ever wanted to be in that place as a career, never ever. It was always a stop gap. It turned out to be an eighteen-year stop-gap, that's not that bad is it?

Were you depressed at work?

Sometimes, I had trouble sleeping but not as bad as it had been. I had five years of serious insomnia... chronic depression. I bought a place in the East End with a girl I used to live with – I met her when I was sixteen or so. She was 24 or 25, six foot, blonde girl. I was like a kid in a sweet shop. She worked with mentally handicapped children. She looked a bit like Glenn Close... She was having affairs behind my back.

Did you wonder what a 24-year-old was doing with a seventeen-year-old? What did your mum and dad make of her?

Obviously, they saw her as a threat. Because I liked her. You get mixed up in your emotions. At seventeen, you think sex is love.

How long did you know each other before you moved in?

Six months or something. I bought a place.

Were you earning quite a bit then?

Maybe about 300 quid a week when I was eighteen. At the time, it was quite good money. We bought a place in Leighton. I didn't like it, it was depressing. It was terrible. She was so possessive. I used to get scratched down my face. It was crazy. She accused me of affairs but it came out it was the other way around.. She lost a child as well. I think both of us ended it in the end. I liked her but the more possessive she got... I think she'd had a tangled past as well. Her dad was a police sergeant and he was quite violent to her. We were together fourteen or fifteen months all told. Then she left. I said I'd take the mortgage over. It went from three or four hundred a month to £600 on my own. It was too much. I used to smoke grass a lot and drink too much. It's terrible stuff. It was only twenty quid a week not Bob Marley scale but I know it does cause psychosis in some people. It certainly didn't help. I was going down hill

Could your mum or anyone help?

I know they were there to help but when my brother had problems she was mortified and I knew she was quite frail and I wanted to protect her... that goes to explain about Ingrid wanting to bring my mum and dad into it.

Perhaps Ingrid wants some affirmation or something?
Well, she's always been unclear about her position with them. She's always felt unease as far as I can tell.

With justification?
No, I think they had open arms – they really liked her but she's not easy-going. I call Ingrid a cross between Elizabeth Taylor and J-Lo. She's not easy-going.

What do you mean: that you think she's a diva?
(laughs) Oh yeah, and a bit like Minelli as well.

You prefer challenging women – you haven't gone for your mother in other words?
(laughs) I always seem to end up with noisy women.

So there you are at eighteen with a mortgage and your heartbroken... or not so much?
No, my illusions shattered, smashed to pieces. I was a little boy emotionally. I used to have relationships one after the other and they never lasted ten minutes; one night stands. All of a sudden living with someone and being a good boy and and after that, self-destructive behaviour. I'd drink until I was shit-faced. I stopped paying the mortgage, partied away.

What happened in terms of your depression?
For five years, I dreaded going to sleep. My mind was racing all the time, non-stop racing. My doctor gave me mild antidepressants –they did nothing. Medium-strength ones. I thought, "Christ, I'm not myself, I'm not taking these." I felt so weird I didn't want to be in the house. I was 22 and really losing it...

Did you talk to mates?
Well, they'd say, "Come on, you depressed again..." You

know, taking the piss. They couldn't understand it. You can imagine what they were like when they discovered I was writing poetry. (*laughs*) Oh, they were delighted... I wrote some terribly depressing stuff. The poems were like a diary. I wrote hundreds. I threw a lot of them away but I can remember ten of the best.

Do you show Ingrid?

I wrote some for Ingrid.

Do you mean she's not interested?

Well, it's hard for her to understand. It's hard for her to understand any play on words, I wouldn't force it on her. I wouldn't force it on anyone. There's one called Alienation that I wrote sometime in 1990. I can't remember the first line..

Did you contemplate suicide?

Yeh, I did. In fact, I took a load of tablets once. I took 40 or 50 tablets and a load of vodka.

It's quite extreme for a young man who comes from a happy home, who looks full of confidence... What did this woman do that was so terrible? Did she bring out the worst in you?

She did bring out the worst in me. My perception of life was shattered.

Did you move back home?

I did. Moving back at 22 or 23 isn't ideal. I was going out all the time, getting better but still behaving in a slightly destructive way. If I went out I was always the one who wanted to stay out all night, that stemmed from the fear of insomnia. Still, now, I stay up late. Sleep deprivation is a torture.

Did it affect work?

I was sick a lot. Always late. Always just on the edge of being in trouble. Two warnings. I was at a football match, Arsenal versus Man U. This guy was drunk, I never even threw a punch. He hit me, so I hit him back, once. Two police men arrested me, I got dragged to the van. I kept asking, "What about the other guy?" They put me in the van, hands behind and feet tied up, neck over the bar. They charged me with assaulting a police officer. How could I when my hands and feet were tied? He was putting a fist to my throat. I remember his face close to mine. I said, "Your mother must be really proud of you..." Still, not learning to shut up (*laughs*) It's pride though, isn't it? They offered me a bound-over to keep the peace but I didn't want to do that. I wasn't guilty. I had my witness and they had two police witnesses and I got guilty and fined £50 for assaulting a police officer. It was just false what they said.

So that was a pretty good start.

(*laughs*) Yeh, I lost my girlfriend, the house, then the police all on top of each other... I thought, what's going on? I remember thinking this has to be intentional. It has to be for a purpose.

You had faith in your powers of recovery?

I always thought that this was designed, well, not designed, but a character building exercise.

What happened next? Were you wary of women?

I was never wary of women. Probably I had low self esteem. I had confidence outwardly. I must've slept with so many girls when I was younger. What's it worth? Nothing. So demeaning.

So how did things improve?

I was still really going down until I was about 25. I had three girlfriends on the trot not long before I met Ingrid.

At the same time?

No, blimey – consecutively. Then I met Ingrid. I was 25-26.

Do you see her as instrumental in cheering you up? Or did she come along at the right time after you were okay?

I was definitely coming back to myself. We met in Shepherds Bush in a night club. She'd been here for a couple of weeks studying. I'd been in the West End with loads of friends and I said, "Come on, we're going to Shepherd's Bush." *(laughs)* Follow me. Quite weird.

Do you mean you think it was fate?

I'd hate to think there was such a thing as fate. I'd hate to think Ingrid was sitting there waiting for me to appear.

She is gorgeous...

Oh yeh, but I'd been out with lots of pretty girls. I knew looks aren't important. Especially since meeting Ingrid I know that (laughs). Obviously it's part of physical attraction but it's so pointless in a way... People say, "Oh, Ingrid is like a film star," and I say, "Yes, but your point is...?"

You say that but there seems a strong affection between you even when you're analysing what's wrong?

I think it really goes deep down. It's too full on. I know her face so well and she's probably the same with me. She's got one of those great open faces, very expressive. I love that. You can communicate so well – or you think you can...

Might you misread things sometimes?

Without a doubt.

It must have been a big risk for you [beginning a relationship

with Ingrid] having gone through the previous trauma?

I must have felt it was right. Our courtship was very strange. She was in Scandinavia. I was London. She had to go back after a couple of months and I felt, "I don't want you to go, uh oh..." I started writing letters.

So it was passionate, moon in June?

I was probably starting to fall in love with her when she went but she'd been involved before. Everyone said it wouldn't work... it would be a nightmare. That made me even more determined. I thought I can do this if I want it enough.

Is that a trait in your personality?

Yeh, I don't think much about astrology but I'm Aries. Hell will freeze over before I give up.

Was she a student?

She'd been working in fashion; a lot of Ingrid's personality is lost in translation. She finds it very difficult to express herself. I have lots of sympathy for that. From my point of view it comes out in frustration, and now we have no communication between us and I like communication. I don't want to be patronising. She's into celebrity and lifestyle, and that to me is the most unimportant thing imaginable. At the beginning she was so upfront, her heart is so much on her sleeve, words are out of her mouth in an instant before it's been processed and I love that. I've never met anyone like that. It's a rare quality. But sometimes, I wish she'd stop and think before she starts. But then again she could say plenty about me.

So how did the romance progress?

We went to Paris, she came here. We went to Rome, lots of dirty weekends, backwards and forwards. Lots of letters going backwards and forwards. I thought of the poem, *Alienation*. "I don't hate anybody/there's just some people I don't understand/I don't love any money/but right now I'd love a grand/I don't value my own life when I think of all the others/But if I should forfeit they could say I'd forgotten my Mothers/ I'm just alive to say good-byes then I've never said hello/and the only friends I've ever had are the ones I'll never know." It wasn't for anyone, it was just what I was thinking. It encapsulated a low point in my life. I felt it can't get any worse – where do I go from here?

Did you and Ingrid decide to live together or get married?

She came over and gave everything up to live with me. [When we first met] I'd scribbled her number down on the back of a fag packet and I could just about read it. I rang and said, "Do you want to come out for a drink?" and she said, "Maybe". I said, "What do you mean? If you want to come out, great but if you don't, I need to know. It's the first date." Then she said, "I think maybe I will". And I thought, "Well, this is different."

Perhaps it's a cultural thing?

It was the same thing again when I asked her to marry me. "Maybe". Then, she said: "Ask me again." And I was quite annoyed. You can't savour the moment twice.

Did you propose to her before she moved in with you?

Yes, we were in Prague.

Had you thought about it or did it just pop out?

I probably did. We were still really, really Superman Krypton stuff. We would row and cry and it was passion all the time. The whole thing was a big fireball all the time, sparks flying off us everywhere we went.

Always right from the beginning a fireball?

Fiery, fiery.

You weren't like that before...?

No, not with anyone else. I phoned her once and said, "Do you like me or love me?" She said, "I l-l-l-I-like you..." I was quite cross. I wrote to her, "If you only l-l-like me, you can f-f-fuck off..." I was quite proud of that.

Do you think you might have pushed her into something?

No, she was in Scandinavia. I just didn't want to be mucked about. If you don't want to marry me don't marry me. So, she decided she was going to come. I said, "If you don't phone me that's fine." She phoned me and said yes. I said, "I'm not going to ask you any more, you're going to have to ask me." So I went to Scandinavia, and she asked me.

I suppose for her it was a much bigger gamble, leaving family, country, friends, job?

Everything. It's pretty incredible. When she came, she said she wasn't going to work for a few months, to get to know the place. I thought, "Oh dear, I'm going on nights because I'm not going to be able to afford this."

Did you say that to her?

Yes I did. I said, if you're not going to be working I'll have to do more overtime in the day, in which case I might as well be on nights. So that's what I did. Obviously, it wasn't something we sorted out properly. So, from day one, we were trying to catch up.

Financially, you mean?

Yes, always.

Is Ingrid good with money?

Good with spending it, but not earning it. We're both not good with money. That's the trouble. It needs one of us. It's descended to a really, really bad way. Recently, I've had a new tactic. Because Dan is growing up in this atmosphere, I can't stand it. I've said to Ingrid if she starts shouting, I'm going to be out of the house. We've got no sex life at all. For a long time, I mean for years. It's just ended. There's no connection. I feel instead, "Oh my God, she's home." It's terrible, there's nothing on the physical side. I'm literally detached from the physical side totally. I don't look at Ingrid anymore and think here comes a beautiful woman. I think here comes that bloody noisy person whom I don't know any more. She probably thinks the same. I think this is the last chance. I'm going to leave her if this isn't resolved. Ingrid says to me, "I know you' re here because of Dan." I love him to death.

At the moment, you're looking after him, are you?

I take him to school. I bring him back. Often I was working late before, so I couldn't put him to bed, read him a story, those kinds of things. She holds all that resentment against me. She didn't say, "You're working hard. I understand that." She always thought I was putting money before the relationship. I said, "Look I have to earn money otherwise we can't pay the bills. We'll never be able to go out." Sometimes, I'd go out in the week, or if I wanted to go out at weekends obviously, because I hadn't seen her in the week, she'd go mad. I'd go to work at two or three in the afternoon and come home at six the next morning. I felt I was living under unreasonable pressure, and she felt she wasn't living the kind of life she would be living in Scandinavia, with a man working nine to five.

So does Ingrid think you're having an affair ?

She does sometimes. I've never had an affair with anyone.

Do you think there's enough between you to revive what you initially had?

I don't know. I don't like this love-hate crap. I want something stable. We're not kids anymore. We need an adult relationship. Aaaagh! It's like she's bubbling... I respond badly to that. I say calm down, and she reacts very badly. She starts screaming and gets very angry. She's clearly very emotional.

Do small things trigger something?

Anything. I'm not brilliant. I don't dust well enough. Ingrid catches the dust before it falls. Ingrid is like a dust fairy.

Isn't that about control, not housekeeping?

I don't know. I remember once her mum lined up all the serviettes so they were the same way. Over perfect. I don't do enough as far as Ingrid is concerned. I don't think I ever could.

What does she say you do well?

(laughs) Get on her nerves. I don't remember her ever giving me a compliment about anything.

Ever?

Ever. And the new business, if I start talking about it, she'll start screaming at me, and say what a load of blah blah, nasty things.

She's trying to undermine you?

All the time. I'm quite confident in what I'm doing so I just take it as ignorance.

At weekends, do you spend time together as a family?

We do. We take Dan to the park. We go to restaurants for lunch a lot. Dinner together.

Do you go out with other couples?

If there's alcohol involved, Ingrid turns. I don't want to sound as if I'm castigating her but I think Ingrid has a problem with alcohol. When she drinks, she just becomes so mean. I've forgotten the number of times we've gone to a party and she's ended up screaming in front of loads of people or getting violent or any number of things. She thinks because we're not having sex, I must be having sex somewhere else. The truth is, I've no sex drive at all at the moment. I think we've had sex twice this year. I can't have a row all day and then say, "Let's go to bed." When she gets pissed, she'll get horny. That's fine but when we've had a row. I can't do that – go away.

Perhaps she's unhappy?

She's deeply unhappy. I don't want to make her unhappy. I really don't want too.

How long ago do you think Ingrid was at her happiest?

I don't know. I met her at the airport, she never comes to give me a kiss ever. I go up to her and kiss her and I get the cheek. I've never found that easy to cope with ever. For Chrissake, I'm married to her.

So you're saying she doesn't initiate affection?

No. She might when she's had a drink or something. But no... I tried to get to the bottom of it – "Something's happened, Ingrid, what's happened?" – to help her and me. I think everyone can benefit from some sort of evaluation. I think this [the book] is fantastic. I'm not worried about it.

CHAPTER THREE
October – Ingrid's first meeting

Ingrid and I arranged to meet after work, away from home, in a hotel in central London. Whereas Tom had taken pains to appear relaxed, Ingrid almost immediately became anxious and emotional. Years of believing that she couldn't make herself heard in the relationship meant that now she talked fast and furiously. At times, she became upset, remembering past and present anger. She was also exasperated by the effort of expressing her feelings in a language that is not her own – although her English is excellent. I heard myself saying, in an attempt to offer comfort, "I'm sure it will get better." But I had no right to say that at all.

***

What did your parents do?
In his twenties, my father worked on cruise ships. Later he was a photographer. My parents divorced when I was about

five. I wasn't so bothered about my father. He hardly ever lived with us and I never got to know him. Sad! I had no feelings for him. For my sister, it was different, she was four years older. He died when I was thirteen and then I was sad. I thought "Now, I'll never get to know him." But then that feeling just went.

How old is your sister?

She's 44. She married at 37 and had three children in five years... very hard work. She has problems sometimes too in her marriage.

What did you want to do at school?

I wanted to go into business and travel. Travel is in the family: my grandmother travelled a lot, my uncle was a pilot. I wanted to travel and live abroad but I always thought I'd settle in Scandinavia. I studied, I had a diploma in business and marketing, that's my background. At 19, I moved from home. I was going out with someone. He was six or seven years older. He was going to come with me, but then I just decided to go.

You mentioned you had an affair with a married man?

He was engaged. He lived about an hour away. We were both keen but neither of us said anything. He was with someone else, what could I say? We saw one another for about two years, then I went to Spain and, when I came back, he'd left his girlfriend and married somebody else. Two years after that, when he also had a child, he wanted to start again but I couldn't.

How did you come to London?

I came in 1995 to do an English course for two months. I met

Tom in the second week. In Shepherd's Bush. I was living there. I was 29. I had a boyfriend in Scandinavia. Tom was young then, he was boyish-looking. Next day he called me and asked me for a drink. (*Laughs*) I said, "Maybe". I wasn't sure. I had a boyfriend who I'd known for two months or so.

Did you tell Tom?

I think so, I can't remember. I didn't want to hurt someone. I was confused by the time I left [England], I knew there was something [between us]... Tom was certain very soon. I couldn't say "I love you" like Tom said to me after two months, I wasn't sure. Tom was writing letters all the time. I just didn't know what to do about this other guy...

It must have been very difficult.

We were commuting backwards and forwards. Tom didn't want to be patient. I thought, "Maybe I should move", then I'd think again, "How can we know each other well before we live together?"

You came here in 1997?

In 1997 after two years. It was a big change. I left my job. I didn't have any money. I had two months off. I didn't know what to do. I got temporary jobs in department stores. I was like a tourist here. I loved it, I still love London. I love its history. Tom was working days, long hours. I didn't mind at first. I had been independent, lived alone for ten years. Tom was very generous, but I'd never lived with anyone before. My mother told me, "I wouldn't do that. I wouldn't give everything up."

Does she like Tom?

Tom makes her laugh. He hugs her a lot, she likes that

because she's very *(Ingrid tenses)*... But they can't communicate. When I complain about cleaning, she says I'm too hard on him. I can get so angry. When we were going away recently I told him to wash his clothes and pack. Nothing happened. Perhaps my expectations are too high. His mum used to do everything. Sometimes, he does it and I do it again. *(laughs)* Cleaning is a big thing in my head. Sometimes I think I can't change myself, but then... It was different before. We had a cleaner. Then he stopped work, and he said he would do it. I don't want to be cleaning when I could be with Dan. I said to Tom, "Why don't we have a Saturday as a family? Why don't we spend time together instead of you going to football every other Saturday?"

The difficulties arose when Tom began working nights?

I told him it's not going to work, we'll end up divorced. You can't sacrifice a family for work. I was on my own, I didn't know many people, I had Dan. I couldn't go anywhere.

What did Tom say?

"Who is going to pay the bills?" He hated the job but his parents didn't want him to leave. They don't like risk. So it was the three of them against me – always. Now in this new business, there's been so many delays. I hope the business does happen but I'm more realistic. I can see how frustrated he is. It was going to start in August, now it's October. He has really bad migraines because of the stress, and his lifestyle. He doesn't exercise *(laughs)*. It would be better if he played football instead of watching it so much! It's been delayed so he's a little bit depressed. I tried to talk to him and maybe I sound as if I'm too critical.

What about weekends now?

We have some weekends together but I have to ask him, stay at home. Why should I have to say that? He has friends who are single, he goes out drinking. They are not family men. He can stay out all night or come home at five in the morning. I do worry about other women but I know he goes to a bloody terrible pub. *(shrugs)*

Do you go out much together?

We haven't been out for a long time. But on Sundays, we go out with Dan to the park or restaurants. When we go out, I have a drink and then I start to complain... blah, blah, blah. I always say that I'm not going to speak about things but then I always do.

Were you like that in other relationships?

I'm not argumentative... only with Tom. [On Saturday] he says he's going to football, so then I say I'm going to the gym for two hours. I wouldn't do it if he wasn't going to football. I never know what's going to happen. I don't ask on Friday, but on Saturday I say what are you going to do? I haven't been to the gym for three weeks, but I like to go because it means I have time for myself. Otherwise it's me and Dan all the time. Tom doesn't understand. Emotionally, we don't speak the same language.

What's Tom like with Dan?

He does a lot for the family. He takes Dan to school. Perhaps my expectations are too high. If we had more interests in common: we don't have anything in common. I wish he would do more sport with Dan. I like a lot of physical things. Tom's different.

What do you like about Tom?

He's faithful and good and optimistic, more than me... I don't think that he has found what he's looking for. I don't think he believes he has succeeded yet in his own life. He believes everything is going to happen when this new business starts, so he can't see beyond that. He's a good man. Sometimes I think we have to learn how to live together because we are very different. Both of us need to learn.

Were you happy together when you were pregnant?

I was happy. Dan was a very easy-going baby. I went back to work when he was one and a half. Now, I feel I don't have any time. It really stresses me out.

Would you like another child?

We have to sort things out before everything but I'd like to have one more.

You said before that you thought that Tom isn't the kind of person you would have chosen in Scandinavia?

Yes... but I don't know. I do feel really, really angry. Sometimes, I feel I could kill him.

Why? Are you saying that you don't think he invests enough time in the family?

Yes, it's quite normal to expect to do things together. Before Tom was working all the time; now he isn't, I say to him, "you look after Dan in the evening, it's your turn. Now, I'm going to make my own time." And he talks about me not being a good mother.

Are you having the same arguments again and again?

I lose my temper quickly... it's small things. He stays at home all day and I come back and there's no soap or toilet paper.

We came back from a weekend away and he left his suitcase downstairs. He doesn't think it's his job to unpack.

Do you mean he has a very traditional view of what a man does in the house?

(nods) I'm so angry with his mum. She does everything. I tell Dan, this is not just women's work.

Is Dan upset by the arguments?

We both tell him, it's nothing to do with you and we love him, but sometimes he says, "Is it my fault?" I think some of the problem is that we are very similar. We're both impatient, strong personalities. He used to be sporty like me but then he had trouble with his knee. He wasn't happy with his job and it affected everything. If he goes out of the house, I text him all the time. Tom is solid and perhaps that's good for me because perhaps I'm not. But then, I look at his family and they don't argue and they never really talk to each other.

Do you mean they don't talk about their feelings?

(nods) When I talk to Tom about my father and family, he understands, he's always on my side. Perhaps some of our problems are to do with my own personal crisis, things coming up from when I was a child, I don't know.

Do you mean that when he goes out, it makes you feel as if you're being left again? Are you worried that he's having an affair?

I wouldn't give him a second chance if he was. Sometimes, I'm suspicious. When he comes in, I check his mobile. I say, "Call this number", and he says "It's just a friend, you call it." I'm not jealous but I'd prefer to know. I want honesty, otherwise bye, bye. I deserve better. I know I do. Deep down,

I think he loves me and I love him. The more I meet couples, the more I realise they have the same problems. It's not love that's the problem, it's living together. Love is the reason but it disappears into so many bad feelings. Sometimes, I look at Tom and I think, "I don't even know you."

Is he still physically attractive to you?

It's not so easy now. Many times I go to bed early. He says, why don't we watch this film together, and I say, I have to be up early for work. It's also difficult when we are arguing.

Would you like to make the relationship work again?

Yes, I would – perhaps in five years time, Tom will be 40 and it will be different. He's younger than me. I told my sister that some of this may bring up things from our childhood. But that's good. We both have to learn.

CHAPTER FOUR

October – Gillian and Penny's first response

At my first meeting with Gillian and Penny, we decided we would report back to Ingrid and Tom as one voice. What emerged was a three-way conversation, with Gillian and Penny contributing their experience and knowledge, and me mostly perplexed and asking questions but adding the occasional opinion. The first mystery, as far as I was concerned, was how two people could live with that level of animosity, however inconsistent, for so long. For Gillian and Penny, that wasn't a mystery at all...

***

The initial impression is that Ingrid and Tom have yet to develop a shared idea of what their marriage is about. They distract themselves constantly – money, his family, football, housework, anger, alcohol – all of which focus attention away from the central issue of how they are going to live together.

Ingrid and Tom also have cultural and family differences which make it more difficult to establish a framework in which they could create a life in common. Tom's parents have been married for a long time with his mother playing a more traditional role. Ingrid comes from a single-parent family, a household of independent women. Tom is perhaps conflicted about what he wants from Ingrid. Most couples develop a script or a narrative about how they each see their relationship. In Tom's narrative, he appears to want a wife like his mother – but he also admires his sister, who seems strong and confrontational. Perhaps this side of Ingrid appeals to him. Perhaps, unconsciously, in choosing Ingrid, he was also tilting at his parents.

At the same time, Ingrid is resisting her husband's idea of what a wife ought to be. She doesn't want to be a wife like Tom's mother, she wants to be herself. This is made more difficult because they do not always "read" each others behaviour accurately. If they can learn to understand each other better, this may lead to more harmony. For example, Ingrid would like Tom to spend more Saturdays with her and Dan. In Ingrid's mind, it is what "normal" families do. At the same time, because of her father leaving the family when she was young, she has a fear both of dependence (hence her reluctance to express her feelings to Tom) and abandonment.

Tom also has insecurities. He is looking for someone who will make him feel safe and will also provide a secure boundary – similar to the boundary provided by his parents that made him happy in childhood. If Ingrid gets angry or rejects him he doesn't feel safe, so he pushes her away and leaves the house. It proves to him that he is still "a free spirit". Ingrid then has her worst fears of abandonment realised. Tom's actions induce Ingrid to pursue him by text and e-mail and mobile. Then he knows he's really wanted, and he also has the boundary he desires set by Ingrid's reaction. So "walking out" has a number of rewards for Tom, some less obvious than others.

When Ingrid asks him to spend Saturdays together, he sees it as controlling, but perhaps she's requesting something that is fundamental to the relationship – a shared life. It might help if Tom could reassure Ingrid rather than enacting what she dreads. Tom is looking for someone who can provide a consistent boundary; Ingrid is looking for a man on whom she can rely. Both are disappointed.

Tom disguises his sense of insecurity by inhabiting different roles – concerned father, dutiful son, perhaps to make reparation for past behaviour? He remains very involved with his own parents. When he expresses concern about Ingrid's drinking, he is perhaps also displaying a fear of his own past tendencies to drink and lose control.

Tom is in a relationship which is full of conflict and therefore very different from his parents' marriage. He needs to explore how to accept constructive conflict in his own relationship. He also appears very compartmentalised – the different elements of his life are kept in separate boxes. Dan and Ingrid are in one box; his parents are in another box; his pub friends are in a third, and so on. This allows him to retain more control in his life – but it is only possible if the boxes remain separate and unconnected.

Tom says he has no choice but to stay out all night to escape Ingrid. But he could choose to stay and attempt to understand what is happening between them and why. Neither Ingrid nor Tom have a clear idea of the compromises and adjustments needed to sustain a relationship and both have difficulties with intimacy. For different reasons, neither saw their parents managing conflict during childhood. Tom's parents rarely argued. Ingrid's father was absent. We made several suggestions. Both should ask themselves if their parents occupy too big a place in their lives. Each could try and view the relationship from the other person's point of view. Each might consider doing something that the other partner requests – which is a departure from his or her own customary behaviour. For example, Tom might ask Ingrid to stay up rather than go to bed early as she usually does, to watch a film together. Ingrid might ask Tom, in turn, to give up football one Saturday. We suggested they try this once over the next four weeks – then choose whether to do it again. We also asked them to write down what happens and how they feel about the challenge of a different pattern of behaviour. Even if they do not succeed, they may learn something. Although Ingrid and Tom have been together for several years, the partnership isn't so much failing as waiting to be forged. What is impressive is that both appear committed.

***

We kept back some observations that might not prove accurate over time or might not be used constructively by the couple at such an early stage. Tom is far more critical of Ingrid than she of Tom. Ingrid appears more reflective of both their behaviour. She is disappointed rather than disillusioned about what the marriage has failed to offer her so far. Ingrid wants Tom to grow up, to stop relying on his mother, be her equal. She wants him to act as her peer but he sees this as nagging so he runs away – a classic theme in many relationships. In turn, Ingrid finds it difficult to assert her point of view. Frustrated, she is quick to anger. She fears both dependency and abandonment so, when he seeks affection, she pushes him away. He misreads this as coldness and/or rejection. They both lack a sense of self, and have not yet married psychologically. In one sense, it's easier for Ingrid. She knows what she wants from Tom – more time spent together, the sharing of life on many levels, an end to Tom's compartmentalised attitude. For instance, Ingrid resents Tom's insistence that their marital problems are kept from his parents. His mother is very involved, and provides a great deal of childcare and often does the family laundry.

Tom, in contrast, appears far more uncertain about what he expects and desires from the relationship. It appears that he wants a bachelor life as a married man. Or has he given up in the face of what he sees as Ingrid's constant demand for a standard of perfection he can never hope to achieve?

If they can shift their deeply held perceptions of each other, focus more on the positive than the negative and examine their own behaviour honestly, they might be able to take the first major step – and agree on the kind of marriage they want to create.

***

A week or so after meeting Ingrid, I made a major error. I emailed Tom a transcript of his interview to his home computer. Ingrid then broke the rules and read what her husband had written. Another major row had ensued. Ingrid said she was happy for Tom to read her interviews, "All I want is openness".

Confidentiality had obviously been broken. Since this might inhibit what Tom said in future, I consulted Gillian and Penny about what we should do. We were, in any case, hardly in a position to issue a red card and send Ingrid off the field. Ingrid, however, was aware how upset Tom had become and expressed both regret and anxiety that the whole process might be abandoned as a result of her action. An action propelled by the notion that Tom must tell the "truth" about her – an idea that she would return to again and again over the coming months, no matter how often we said that all truth is subjective. What particularly concerned her was that she was not expressing herself adequately in a second language – although I found her very eloquent at times.

We took Ingrid's regret as a good sign that she was committed to the process. Whether or how this breach would affect Tom's willingness to talk, we would have to see.

CHAPTER FIVE
Ingrid's story

I was born in 1964. My mother was in her twenties when she had us. My dad came from a family who were more upper class than my mum's family and had a servant, which was not so common at that time. My paternal grandmother was quite religious. Though she never pushed her religion on to us, I certainly got to know God and I felt blessed in many ways. I still do. I believe in God and know that there is somebody watching and protecting us.

My father went through quite a bad time after the divorce. Alcohol was very much in the picture. That was one of the main reasons my mum left him. My mum's parents weren't happy at all about his behaviour and I guess they encouraged my mum to divorce. They must have thought we could manage better without him. He was not there often anyway.

In his thirties, my father stopped drinking, got married again and had two more children and started a fashion business. He also found religion. He gave many magazine interviews about his life and how he had found peace... Earlier, he had been successful, but his drinking took its toll in the end. He said that people always saw him as confident but inside he was anything but. He had low esteem (so I heard) and it didn't help that there was always cheap alcohol available on the ships in which he sailed.

I think he enjoyed being in the public eye [as a celebrity photographer] He had a lot of charisma. He was also very good in business. People liked him. He died at the age of 49 on a skiing holiday in Lapland. It was a heart attack. I was then fifteen or sixteen. I felt very sad, mostly because I realised it was too late to get to know him better. Otherwise, his death didn't change our everyday life at all. I got over his death quite quickly. Or so I thought...

We were my mum's first priority after the divorce. She needed to work full time so my grandma looked after us during the day. There were many women around, my mum, her sisters and both my grannies. All of them were very feminine women but very strong characters, and independent. They obviously put their own stamp on me. My grandmother and my aunties spoilt us but we didn't get everything we wanted as money was tight. My mum was very imaginative and we always had good clothes etc. at school. I never felt unfortunate. However, it was never easy for me to accept that I didn't have a dad. I always avoided that subject with other people. I couldn't face that fact that my dad had left my mum and us. Why? Now I am asking the same question about Tom... I feel like he has left me, too. We could have been such a perfect family. In my own dream world, I always wanted a proper family. My dream between the ages of ten and fifteen was to become a nanny.

My mum must have felt devastated after the divorce. However, I never saw her unhappy. I can't remember her mentioning my dad. I can't blame her for that. My dad just didn't existed in our life. It was better that way – or was it? He visited us sometimes and once I remembered that I left the house to avoid him. I wasn't ready to meet him. I was about thirteen. My mum had some boyfriends but never serious ones... or if she did I didn't know about them. She travelled quite a lot with her friends and sisters (and with me when I was 25 to 30) and enjoyed her life. But sometimes I think she has lots of stuff inside that she she has not poured out... Sometimes when we speak about him she bursts into tears.

My sister was more sensitive than me in a way but very strong as well. She went through her childhood experiences with a counsellor once. She experienced and remembered much more than I did. I never felt that I could speak to n outsider about my past. However, I discussed those feelings with my mum many times. I think I was closer to my mum than my sister was.

I met my proper first love when I was 18. He was ready to settle down and move together. I was not. My life had just started. Next, was a man who was eight years older than me. I was 24-25. He took my breath away. I knew instantly he was the man for me. Sadly he was not free at the time [he was engaged and living with his girlfriend]. It didn't matter, I was in love with him, though I knew it was wrong. I ended that affair after two years. I left for Spain for six months. When I came back he had met a new woman. I felt as if I'd died...

However, after three years he wanted to see me again. I was engaged to Tom but we did meet and I poured everything out, my feelings about him, all the emotions, how I had felt after leaving him... I knew that he still had feelings for me. But I left in both our interests. I was proud of myself and somehow relieved. That was the end of one era.

After him I had a relationship with a married man for some time. He became quite serious about us so I ended it. I told him that I wasn't going to break up his marriage.

Before I came to London for an English course I had been going out with a man for about six months. He was ready to start a family. I decided I needed to brush up my English. I had ambitions. When I told him about my plans, it was the end for us even though we didn't say it out loud.

Almost all my men seem to have had something in common. They were older than me, had a sense of humour, and business ability, they lived away or were attached to somebody else. They were sensitive and sentimental characters even though they put up a tough front. I guess I held myself back quite a lot. I don't think my boyfriends knew how to handle me. They sometimes weren't sure about my feelings. I couldn't easily express my emotions unless I was 100 per cent sure about the feedback. But then, often, they weren't free... an impossible situation. I am still very straightforward and impatient. I get bored easily and need stimulation and total openness from a man. That is very important.

Then I met Tom. He was younger than me, boyish-looking, beautiful eyes, good kisser (very important!) and lots of humour. I felt that I could trust him even though I did not know him so well. I loved London. I felt free and enjoyed every minute. Our relationship was quite passionate. Lots of going out, strong emotions, sex... It was fun and I felt a teenager again.

After two months I went back home. I didn't think it would last. I was really touched by his letters (and poems) but didn't know what to do. We continued to seeing each other whenever possible, in Paris, Rome and of course in London and Scandinavia. It was fun but it wasn't easy... After a year we got engaged and the decision was taken that I would come to London. I had a year's leave of absence from my job and took a risk. Was it worth of it? I am still here, so...

Dan was born by a Caesarean section. All my birth plans about natural birth, etc, went out of window. He was lovely and I felt happy. Soon after coming home from the hospital I developed an infection. I was in and out of hospital because the antibiotics didn't work. I was ill for the first time in my life and it took some time to recover. Mentally I was fine. I have always had a positive attitude towards life. That helped.

I finally got better. My mum stayed here for three months. and Tom's mum helped a lot, too. Dan was very good baby and slept very well. I loved being a mum. But sadly I soon felt as if I was a single mum. Tom and I did not go anywhere together. I was knackered.

I got lucky and landed a good job with decent hours and brilliant colleagues. I felt appreciated and I found my self-esteem again. We not only spoke the same language, we also shared the same background, culture etc... I was good old Ingrid again (at work at least). Tom was really happy and proud of my new job too.

Our marriage then hit rock bottom.

I started to go out more often without him and felt happier. It was good for me. Tom's mum used to look after Dan when I was out. Tom was still working long hours. However, I did not want to go out during the weekend because I felt we ought to be together at least then. Tom didn't agree and he often went out on both Saturday and Sunday.

I felt so empty, alone, angry, betrayed, rejected. Still do. I felt sorry for Dan too. I couldn't understand how any parent or husband could behave like that. I felt I had failed and I must be terrible person, wife, mother, as he often told me I was. Tom just continued to live his own life, in a bubble, with his own rules.

As I was at home at weekends, I had a glass or two, or the odd bottle of wine during a meal to relax. It caused a lot of quarrels. All I heard was that I had a drinking problem, how aggressive I was, etc. He couldn't see beyond his problems and why I was shouting or behaving in that way. He always said it was due to my period or PMS or I was moody or drunk. Without Dan I would have gone a long time ago. But if we did leave, I don't know where I'd go.

I feel the same as I did five years ago: angry, bitter, lonely mentally and physically (he has banned sex from me for many years) So there is no closeness between us and I no longer regard him as attractive. Maybe I need a lover? I don't think Tom would mind.

Dan is the most important thing in my life and I am so proud of him. I know the situation cannot continue like this. He is an innocent little boy and should not be seeing this... I can't always take account of his feelings because I am so heartbroken and lost myself. I really hate myself when I loose my temper with Tom or Dan. Sometimes Tom sees me behaving like this and I think he believes he should leave for Dan's sake... I feel insane. This is not me. All my energy goes into arguing with Tom – I can't stand him at home. Maybe because I know that he doesn't want to be at home.

I know I would be devastated if he said he's leaving... but in the end it may be for the best? But I don't want my son to go through the same trauma as I did [losing a father]. I am also worried that Dan sees me so unhappy, which is not my true personality. I would do anything to make our life better.

I am very glad we met you to have this chance. I hope everything will be better one day, one way or other.

Chapter Six

All you need is love...?

It's called the glass slipper syndrome: the belief that all it takes is Prince Charming, and the right size foot in the shoe, and love will deliver the rest. Except, of course, love is never enough. Tom refers often to his parents' successful 40-year marriage. If they did it – why can't he? Ingrid, in spite of her desperation at the state of their relationship, also talks warmly about the happy times she and Tom had "courting". He had pursued her, certain he had found "the one". At a slower, more hesitant pace, she had come to the same conclusion. So how and why had it soured so quickly?

In the past 30 years, the divorce rate has trebled and the number of marriages has halved. Cohabitation, which brings with it a far higher rate of break up, is on the increase. Marriage is falling out of favour but surveys tell us that what most people still want is a partner for life.

Yet the odds against this happening are stacking higher and higher. Roles within marriage were once far more defined, moulded by cultural and religious conventions and bound by obligation. Couples stayed together because of their religious beliefs, notions of respectability and economic necessity. A personal sense of obligation to stick it out, "for the sake of the children", was also much more prevalent. The wife did all the housework, childcare and domestic organisation; the husband was the head of the house and the breadwinner. He brought home the bacon; she cooked it. Divorce was frowned upon and a woman without a man found it hard to survive. Unsurprisingly, some couples found themselves in holy deadlock, stuck with each other in mutual animosity, until death finally prised them apart.

Others fared better, and some much better. Couples may have lived parallel lives (her at home; him at work) but, on occasions (births, marriages, deaths – Saturday night in the pub) they would rub along together, appreciative of the fact that they were part of a team. In some relationships, tolerance, respect and companionship reinforced a sense of partnership. Sex – with many exceptions – may not have been stellar but these modest terms, supported by the web of the extended family, often sustained what was considered a good marriage. Then, personal happiness was only one of a number of considerations that kept a couple together – now it's the holy grail. Western marriage, once forged by external restraints, moral, religious and social, now relies in many cases only on self-restraint.

Today, the majority of those who marry do so in their late twenties. They may enjoy an extended honeymoon period and then, often shortly after the arrival of children and those long, sleep-starved nights, they enter the tricky waters which will decide whether they'll separate (at 38, on average for a woman; at 40 for a man) or stay together.

And, while the rules of matrimony are no longer clear, the expectation of what love is supposed to deliver is much higher. Women, for instance, no longer need a husband for respectability, status, children or income – or because of what the neighbours might say if you are 35 and still minus a man. They have grown pickier. If surveys are any guide, it is possible to draw up a common wish-list of what each gender believes constitutes the ideal partner.

The majority of women, it seems, seek an attentive lover, best friend and life coach in one. A man who is at ease with his own feelings, unafraid of intimacy and an unending source of passion, affection and esteem. A person who shares their values, and values their share of the relationship, instead of taking it for granted. A man who wants a life in common but who doesn't complain when his wife or girlfriend demands a semi-detached life of her own (though she doesn't necessarily want him to have one too).

And what do men seek? Humour, affection, companion-ship, respect, good sex and, among younger men, equality (in theory if not in practice – since women still take on the majority of the domestic and childcare duties). Polls indicate that men appear to have more luck than women in find-ing a soul-mate. In a 1997 NOP poll 71 per cent of men said they would definitely marry their partner again; only 56 per cent of women agreed.

Couples today negotiate on a daily basis who does what

and when, whose needs have priority, how much time apart is healthy, how much time together is wise, while all the time the message pumped out by popular culture is that deception, disloyalty and adultery is the norm. Generations have been reared on the television soaps' depiction of romance in which the three dominant characteristics are predatory sex, anger and betrayal.

Some couples replay the same argument, word for word, umpteen times a month, year in year out – a ritual that is harmful to themselves and frequently to their children too. They prefer the security of this destructive routine to the unknown danger that may come from unravelling the causes and finding a resolution that either shifts the relationship to a better place, or brings it to a conclusion. Today all too often we require our lovers to be our saviours. We expect them to make us happy even though, in some cases, we have failed to make ourselves happy when single.

Even in the darkest moments, many couples claim they want to make a success of their relationship, but they don't know how to break the habit of combat. Nine out of ten couples resist going to counselling for all sorts of reasons, including the fact that both individuals, not just one, have to acknowledge the relationship is in trouble.

And yet long-term couples testify that the good times are made even better precisely because of how the bad times have been weathered. Why do so few of us manage to learn from their experience? For many, "working" on a marriage is itself seen as an admission of failure. Love is supposed to be all you need.

Those who do seek help often leave it too late – on average, six years too late. Some couples stay together but are permanently paralysed by misery, often from the first years of their relationship. Or they divorce after years of unhappy matrimony only to find that the conflict re-emerges in a new partnership. They have left a marriage but taken some of their reasons for its breakdown with them... Love, in fact, is rarely enough.

Even if couples gain some insight into their problems, they can be difficult to correct. Relationships are soured not just by internal domestic affairs but often by family history, as well as external pressures like stress and work anxieties and constant demands on time. One clear message that recent research delivers is that a strong relationship is *made*, not found. The greater the baggage we bring to a relationship, the tougher the challenge in fashioning something worthwhile. As writer Adrienne Burgess explains in *Will You Still Love Me Tomorrow?*, "Becoming the right person in a relationship is as important as finding the right person."

According to research, those who are fatalistic ("If it does-n't work out, we can always get a divorce"), may believe they have no power to resolve difficulties when they arise.

Research also tells us that high quality, long-lasting relationships have never been easy. Long-term couples experience, over the years, a kind of matrimonial Mexican wave. They have an attitude of mind and an ability to focus on the positive aspects of why they are together which pulls them through the dark periods until they reach a high again. Robin Gutteridge, in her research on long-term couples in the UK, says these relationships go through three stages: testing, building and maturing. Once they reach the maturing stage, the relationship moves from one that requires investment to a resource which is drawn on for mutual and individual needs. It releases energy, recharges interest and encourages confidence.

Interestingly, while unhappy couples relate very different narratives of their life together, content couples who have spent decades together tell a similar story when they are interviewed separately. According to sociologist Linda J Waite and journalist Maggie Gallagher, major figures in the American pro-marriage lobby in *The Case for Marriage,* long-term marriages offer better sex, better health, better income, better self-esteem and greater emotional well-being, as well as giving children a sound anchor in life.

Religious faith often plays a vital role in persuading couples to stay together. Couples without a faith and only their own belief that a marriage will improve have far more fragile unions. But even that is changing. In 1972, American sociologist Jessie Bernard described "his and her" marriages. His marriage was better than hers. The wife suffered from exhaustion, mental ill health and a loss of a sense of self. The husband, cared for, nourished and set free of all worries so he could concentrate on his career and his hobbies, flourished.

Feminists took up the cause: marriage was bad for women. A Sally Ann Lasson cartoon has one man saying to the other, "Who on earth is happily married ?" "I am," the second man replies. "Yes," responds the first, "But your wife isn't."

Marriage has, of course, become a political battle ground

because it has its roots in the oppression of women. The Right is traditionally pro-marriage; the Left is often a passionate advocate of the "good" divorce and cohabitation. In this context, hidden agendas are sought in every piece of research, a scepticism that unfairly reduces too many valuable findings to the level of propaganda.

Every study has an element of the subjective – how are participants selected? What questions are asked? What variables are overlooked or perhaps under-emphasised? Taking all these qualifications into account, nevertheless, an ever growing body of evidence is delivering a similar message: marriage works, even for women. Marriage, as an institution, does offer positive benefits, as yet unmatched by cohabitation or a life alone. It gives what Dr Jack Dominian, the Godfather of relationship research in the UK, called "an ordered belonging". No matter how many unattached 30 and 40-somethings say they love their single life, recent research confirms that those with the greatest sense of well-being are the married, followed in descending order by cohabitees, then those who are dating steadily, followed by casual daters and, lastly, those at the bottom of the well-being scale are individuals who date infrequently or not at all.

The study conducted by American academics Paul R Amato and Claire M Kamp Dush, published in the *Journal of Social and Personal Relationships*, defines "subjective well being" as a state that positively affects people's mental and physical health, their sexuality and their financial status, and permits them to have a favourable view of themselves and their lives. Well-being embraces self-acceptance, positive relations with others, autonomy, purpose in life, personal growth and low levels of negativity – much of which is the direct antithesis of the lives Ingrid and Tom are living at present.

But what gives married people higher levels of well-being than single people? Research shows that "love" is only a fraction of the answer. Until recently, many researchers into matrimony argued that selection mattered. Well-adjusted individuals are more likely than poorly adjusted people to get married and stay married. In other words, it's not marriage that works the magic – but the kind of people it attracts. Amato and Dush reject this view. They say that the evidence of "hundreds of studies", indicates that it's the institution itself and the benefits it may bring that generates well being. For instance, evidence shows that becoming part of networks of long-term support – as, say, part of your husband or wife's extended family – not only improves emotional and physical health, it also acts as a buffer against the hard times, when facing, for example, redundancy or illness.

Another reason why marriage improves well-being also provides a possible clue as to why Ingrid and Tom have hung on to their increasingly threadbare relationship for so long. According to research, an individual will put up with a poor quality marriage because the institution itself, crucially anchored in commitment, supports the range of roles that makes up that person's life – spouse, partner, friend, sibling, employee, parent.

These roles are organised hierarchically with higher order roles contributing more to people's core identities than lower order roles. Roles that have a high level of commitment make especially strong contributions to people's sense of self. So, no matter how fractious day-to-day living, for some, the "reward" that comes from being a spouse is infinitely preferable to an alternative role as a divorcee or unattached adult. "Even individuals in relatively unhappy marriages may benefit from the stability, commitment and social status of marriage," Amato and Dush write, "[while] the long-term horizon of marriage may provide people with the hope that their relationships will improve in future."

Hope, in the case of Tom and Ingrid, isn't exactly in plentiful supply – but it exists.

CHAPTER SEVEN

November: Tom's second interview

Tom and I met in the same hotel. The bar was again deserted except for Terry Wogan and a colleague taking tea in a far corner – all of which somehow added to the sense of the surreal. I was slightly apprehensive about Tom's reaction, having read his own transcript and our first report and knowing that his words had been read by Ingrid – might he be inclined to call the whole experiment off? Instead, he was gracious about my error. What emerged, however, made me think that, instead of improving the marriage our efforts, so far, had only served to deepen the wounds.

***

I'm really pissed off about it, [Ingrid reading the transcript of Tom's first interview] I really am at the moment.

What about the suggestion of putting yourself in each other's shoes?

We've only just started talking yesterday. She said I shouldn't have said those things. That's the ultimate sort of betrayal in a way, saying to me after reading that report, "Why don't you go and kill yourself, it's your fault that for the last five years we're not having sex." It's true, I must have loads of psychological baggage left over from those things that I went through, but to have it all chucked at you like that… I actually went and bought *Loot*, I was going to get a flat… but then I thought how can I do it without affecting Dan? I don't want to take that step because I probably won't come back.

Ingrid knows that you were going to do that?

She had four hours of a tantrum while she was hoovering, just screaming and shouting while Dan was here, and I just said, "Right if you don't stop, I'm going to go," and she stopped. I went and bought *Loot* and I sat in the café and marked out a few places, I think she saw it and maybe it was me letting her know as well. I didn't say anything to her, but she came and gave me a kiss and ended it. I just thought, "Oh right." I'll take any excuse not to go anyway, it wouldn't take much to persuade me to stay, a smile or something like that.

So you still really strongly want to try and get it on an even keel?

I would try but at the same time, I'm really sometimes losing the will to do it. She has to be careful because it's Dan I'm thinking of, but there has to come a time when you just sort of say no.

One of the things that Gillian and Penny said was they felt that on both sides…

The relationship hadn't been forged. I found that interesting, I did find it all interesting. I wouldn't call it criticism because it's not, and I look at it positively, I don't look at it as a criticism at all.

I wonder if you working nights, for example, might have been partly because you were anxious about getting involved in a relationship – maybe not consciously?

Well, no, to be honest with you, that was purely a monetary reason. We were having a normal relationship before but obviously we went downhill quickly. She said to me, the reason she didn't kiss me at the airport when she saw me was because I didn't have the right T-shirt on, or she didn't like my T-shirt or something like that. If you're going to be so sensitive or so outrageous, that's why I call her diva. She really hated that. I think that's what really wound her up the most.

Why do you think that was?

That really hit home, I don't think she sees herself like that. I know she means well, she's got such a great heart you know, she really has. She's so honest and her heart is on her sleeve, it's just some of the stuff she thinks about isn't processed properly. It just comes flying out in an emotional blur.

What if you did what Gillian and Penny said and, for example, didn't go to football this Saturday?

I would definitely do those things, that's no problem. Ingrid said I go out Saturday and Sunday. She would not be able to say to you that I've ever done that, ever.

So why do you think she's saying it?

Because she was just angry when she wrote that, I think.

Or maybe what she's saying is…

Football is more important than…?

You're not present in the family.

Yes.

That you're living your life.

Yes.

Gillian and Penny said you tended to compartmentalise your life.

I don't want to say they're wrong but I have my own view about that. I don't know why but I have friends who, for one thing or another, are different to each other and they wouldn't necessarily be able to mix but if you could find someone who was – in my case, who loved poetry, or someone who liked the same interests as me, who liked to talk about the same things I did, then they would be with you on all levels and they would be a soul friend, wouldn't they? But you can only meet someone like that really, maybe once in your life. So that's why I put things in compartments because you can't possibly say that someone is the whole thing to you.

What about Ingrid, couldn't she become that soul mate?

Yes, why not, of course. I didn't marry Ingrid for… I thought I might have come across as quite destructive when I was talking about looks and things like that, which is a bad thing. But I didn't mean it like that. I didn't marry Ingrid for her looks, for her money, for her background, for her conversation, for her anything – I married her because I loved her. It wasn't anything else, it was just purely because of that and that was enough and it's always going to be enough for me. Now I might be wrong in thinking that's enough but I still do, and I will always think that.

When you say, "that's enough"?..

We have to build on that, but it should be enough if we've got a strong relationship.

It's a question I suppose of how you build on it isn't it?

Yes, that's true, that really is the question. Sometimes I don't want to, and then sometimes I see her laugh and smile, a genuine moment, and I really think, yeah, I want to again. It just takes that one moment of something and it's amazing, it really is, you know. It's just strange, but Ingrid's so difficult... funny but difficult in a way.

Presumably because of the state of your relationship, it's probably made her even more sensitive?

She's always been like this, before we even got really, deeply involved, she's always been like this, just so panicky.

One of the things they said was about both of your relationships with your parents.

Ingrid really resents my parents. She's just got so much anger towards my parents, I think because she's sees it's their fault that I'm not Mr All-singing, All-dancing, All-cleaning man. Ingrid even says it herself, since I haven't been at work, I've been cooking, cleaning for Dan. I go shopping with him two or three times a week, we go to get vegetables, bring them back, wash them, peel them together and make juice and all that. I'm doing all those things and her attitude is, "So what? I've been doing that for five years." That seems to be a common theme. I've done it for five years, I have to put Dan to bed every night now and I'm thinking, "Well, no, you put him to bed sometimes as well Ingrid, because you have to read to him as well" – and she says, "Well, I've been doing it

71

for five years." I think, "for God's sake, not that again."

I suppose what she's asking for is some kind of reparation isn't she? She's trying to say, I don't know...

Vengeance it seems like to me.

If both of you can be more constructive... I know it is really difficult but it's this thing about winning all the time I suppose, isn't it?

What, both of us too competitive, you mean?

Yes, if both of you agreed to the other's point of view. I know that sounds really difficult.

I understand what you're saying...

She's miffed about that first five years... what's done is past, but what else can...?

What can I do – yes, I've said to her what do you want me to do? The time's gone, the time's past. I've got better in some ways, obviously since I've changed my job.

Just go back to your relationship with your parents, what did you think about Gillian and Penny saying they may still play quite a large – perhaps disproportionate – role in your life?

I don't see that, I think parents should play a role, an important role... I didn't have a good relationship with my dad for a long time. When I was younger we had a terrible time. I didn't really appreciate the sort of person he was until I got a lot older. So we've forged a relationship fairly recently, in the last few years.

When you say you didn't have a good relationship, was that all through your childhood?

No, it was just when I got to teenage years, which I suppose is fairly typical. Just last year, me and my dad went to see where he was born in Dublin and where he grew up, and that was important. I don't think Ingrid fully understands.

She hasn't known a father has she?

Well, no, it's incredibly difficult for her but she seems to think it didn't matter. But she says that when he died, she was really sad and so obviously that just tells you two stories doesn't it? To me it shows that she was incredibly sad that she never had a father in the first place.

But people quite often have two stories, don't they – I'm not a counsellor – but you have a story that you tell the rest of the world as a defence, and then you have a story that you tell yourself. One of the things that she seems to be doing is recognising now how much the absence of a father had an impact?

That's true, that's beautifully summed up.

But somehow that has to be something that doesn't stand between you but is a link. Because at the moment it's standing between you isn't it?

Possibly, yes. I don't know why she should feel resentment to my family.

She really likes your family.

Hmmm – she does say that but every time there's a real argument, she'll say, "Oh, your bloody mum" and "Dan's allowed to do this at your mum's house and that's why he's doing that…" Maybe she feels Dan is too close to my mum or something. I've encouraged it. I didn't have grandparents when I was a child. I just love that relationship that Dan's got, and a different relationship than he's got with me. Why shouldn't he enjoy his grandparents? I know that Ingrid's probably feeling bad because her mum can't be here for Dan as well. But that's different to having a problem with my mum, I don't understand that. We're very different. My dad, for example, when he was growing up, it was very difficult. He lived in Dublin in the 1950s, it was real poverty.

Angela's Ashes **stuff?**

Real poverty… the infant mortality rate was obviously chronic and so was the… imagine it now, the epidurals that woman have now. [Talks about birth of Dan] Ingrid was saying "I'm going to have a natural birth." I said "I'm with you, whatever you want to do… it's your birth, not mine". She was actually in labour 24 hours, and she still remembers the half hour I was asleep and not the 22 I was there. Blimey, I didn't even leave the room. Ingrid was such a pain. I just felt so guilty because she was being a bloody nightmare. She was shouting and screaming, obviously in real pain. So I actually got one of the nurses outside and I said my wife's finding it difficult. It's her first child, really just be firm with her. It was a big tough Irish midwife and [she said to Ingrid] "You're not the first one to have a baby, you won't be the last, get on the bed – no messing around…" Ingrid had a terrible time [after the birth]. I was so disgusted with the hospital. She was just getting antibiotics and coming out again, going in again. I said to the sister, "There's no way she's coming out of hospital until you sort it out." So they gave Ingrid her own room and then sorted it out properly.

And who was looking after Dan?

My mum and me. It was a really, really tough time for her. Ingrid was a different person after that, I think it really changed her.

In what sense was she different?

I don't know, I think she became very… I don't know, I saw a more cynical Ingrid after that definitely.

Why do you think that would have been the case?

Well, I'm not sure. I don't know if she was prepared for what she went through. Who could have been? It was a traumatic time for her, it really was, no doubt about that, it really was… Christmas in hospital, and over New Year.

Very hard isn't it when you've got a dream of how something should be and the reality's different?

Yes, Ingrid was going to have a natural birth, no painkillers. Me, I'd like gas… the whole lot – have you got any more? But a natural birth went straight out the window. When I was a kid, I remember my mum in the early 70s saying to me, there's a Nigerian lady moved in down the road, why don't you go and say hello to her, her son is called Billy. I look back on it now and think, blimey, how many people in those times would have done that? My mum used to do Christmas dinners for the old ladies in the street and all that, and I think it's brilliant. My dad was illiterate and he taught himself to read and write basically and he's got a whole book of chemical symbols that he wrote and drew himself and he's into cosmology. He's a fantastic brain about astronomy, cosmology. He's a member of the British Astronomical Association. He's a brilliant chess player, draughts player, won cups and medals for those things.

So you admire him a lot?

Yes, I do. He's a jazz encyclopaedia, play him jazz or a classical piece of music and he can tell you who wrote it and probably what colour boxer shorts they had on. It's incredible but he's unassuming. My mum as well. I became friends with this kid Billy from Nigeria until he was about fourteen or fifteen – best mates, which was fantastic. Actually, my dad had loads of black friends when he was in his job and obviously at the time, there was lots of racism. My dad never had that at all and I've never had it.

In a way I suppose, because you talk about your dad so vividly does that help you to understand Ingrid's relationship with her father?

I won't minimalise the importance of my parents to me. At the same time, I don't think they – if Gillian and Penny say they are too important, I don't understand in what way because I think they're role models to Dan and I think that's very important.

What about the question of boundaries, you want to feel secure, but because of the way the relationship is at the moment, that doesn't happen, so you leave and that reinfores what Ingrid feels?

Yes, the abandonment theory. It's something I've thought about before from Ingrid's point of view but I don't really know how we're going to deal with it. I don't want Ingrid to feel abandoned, ever. At the same time, I *feel* as though it's probably not for me to address that problem, it's for her to address the cause of it.

I suppose if you're physically gone though, that doesn't help much does it?

Yes, but in that case, we should just say, cure the symptoms by me not making her feel abandoned, or should we try and address why she feels abandoned in the first place.

Both?

Well, exactly, I feel it should be two-pronged. I couldn't give a toss about football to be quite honest with you, since football seems to be coming up a lot [with Gillian and Penny]. I go out to get out of the house, to kind of escape.

It's not actually just about football. If you're going to spend time together at the weekend... perhaps Ingrid might see you in the morning to sit down and work out what you're going to do for the rest of the day. I don't know how it works?

Yesterday, I took Dan to a Halloween party and Ingrid was nursing the mother of all hangovers. I mean she was really, really drunk. The worst I've seen her. I was just so pissed off about it. She went out all day Saturday which is – I'm absolutely cool with it, I say to her, go out with your friends. She said she was going out with a couple of friends for a birthday... She went from about two in the afternoon, and then about seven pm Dan and I phoned her and said good-night. She said, I'll be coming home soon. I said, "Yeah, yeah, when you want." Because she always says that and she always stays till three in the morning. I always say to her, "Don't come home pissed on the train, come home in a black taxi, I'll pay if you haven't got the money... don't worry about what it's going to cost... just get home." So, two o'clock in the morning, I get a phone call completely incoherent. "Where are you – where are you?" Dan was asleep, I couldn't leave him alone to pick her up, no way... and the phone went dead and now I'm really worried. So I phone her about twenty times, no answer again, texting her, phoning her, I'm really,

really worried now. I can't sleep, it's about three or four in the morning. She comes home and I was waiting for her. I was literally standing at the window thinking, I hope she's alright because she was so messed up. I was really annoyed at her friends, because you're supposed to look after each other and get each other into taxis.

You know who her friends are?

Yes. Anyway, I saw her staggering and falling from one side of the pavement to the other. She came in and she'd got blood on her forehead and on her nose where she's fallen over. The next day she was mortified. She didn't remember what happened. She tried to say it was the bus doors or something. I gathered she was on her own and she got the bus and she couldn't walk. She couldn't come upstairs for hours. She was literally comatose. I said I'm really getting worried about you, I didn't get to sleep until about six o'clock in the morning. Next day I've never seen her so remorseful, very guilty. I said, "Don't worry about it – so long as you got home."

So you can have conversations with each other?

Yes, but I'm frightened of starting a conversation because it's just going to go off. So much shouting, that's what I can't abide. I really can't abide the shouting.

But unless you do start taking that risk, both of you.

Well, we've done it for so long. If we start having deep conversations, it would end up with Ingrid screaming. Not me screaming, it would end up with Ingrid screaming and I'm sorry to say that's not my fault because I've tried to have... conversations but I feel Ingrid is the one who will blow it all up. That's why I'm really grasping at this because we're not capable [of change] together.

What do you think might encourage her not to yell?

I don't know. If I agreed with everything she said, it would be very easy, because if you don't agree with Ingrid then you're wrong basically, there's no debate. For those first five years didn't she ever notice that while I was working nights, she didn't have to pay any bills? Did she never notice that?

Did you not bring it up?

Oh yes, of course, but you don't get points… even if you're doing something that they benefit from. I was earning about £30,000 a year, five years ago. You can't just walk out of a job and go straight to another job earning £30,000. I'll give you an example, I went for a job in an estate agency. I did loads of research. I was one of the last people to interview. The interviewer said, "I've interviewed 50 already". So I thought, Oh Christ, that doesn't sound very good and he put me in the middle of the estate agent's to do the interview. So I just, really-ly went for it. I got a phone call saying, "Fantastic, blew me away, I want you to start blah blah blah…" I was really over the moon – "Ingrid, I've got this job!" It was £17,000 plus commission and car. I did the sums and I couldn't take it.

When you read your own interview did it strike you…

What came out? I remember when I talked to you about the suicide thing, I've never talked to anyone about that before. Ingrid wrote in her e-mail that she already knew all these things – she really didn't. I'm basically talking to a stranger about things I've never opened up to her in that way. I think that probably really hurt Ingrid as well, whereas I'm not like that. I read things I didn't know about Ingrid. Well, I probably knew them but they didn't phase me, about her visiting her exs and stuff. Fine, that's the way it is. That's past life isn't it? I'm not quite so hung up on those things, I'm quite broad-minded.

It's interesting that, as she said, she's quite often chosen unattainable people?

Yeah. Ingrid is destructive in this relationship and I probably am as well, but then it's like the irresistible force and the immovable object isn't it? We were always going to be flames and sparks weren't we?

Why do you say that?

Well, I'm not saying it's a pre-written destiny, but it just seems as though from our rows...

Do you think this process is making it worse?

I expect that to happen. I'm prepared for probably a lot worse still. Going back to when I read my report, what did I think – I remember about the suicide thing. I remember I actually went to two different chemists and bought two packets of those tablets. I was lying in bed next to her and I'd taken the tablets in the bathroom and I'd buried the packets in the bottom of the bin, and the wrapper. She jumped up. I was going to sleep and she said, "You've done something," and she woke me up and said, "If you don't go and make yourself sick, I'm going to call an ambulance." She took the bin out and found them at the bottom. I was sick and I remembered this white foam, just loads of white foam came up. She was just hysterical. I remember thinking to myself, my God what did you do? Once I'd written that poem, I knew that I'd sort of rationalized it in my head. I would never do that again.

That was really a turning point.

I'm seeing you today and Ingrid tomorrow. In a practical way what will you do for each other? What can you do for her?

Well, we aren't on speaking terms. We've had no communication.

Dan must know or sense.

Well, I don't know how he doesn't. He's just such a good lad. I really don't want to put him through any of this at all. Once, she was shouting and she said, "It's good that Dan can hear that I'm angry. It's good that Dan can hear why I'm pissed off with you." She was screaming, and I told her, "I don't care what you say to me, I don't care how you say it but why do that in front of him? Why do you have to shout in front of Dan?" I find it unbelievable that she's actually pleased to use Dan as a weapon. In some respects I would hate her forever for doing that.

You can't hate her forever and then try and improve the relationship.

I just want her to stop doing that. If she stops doing that, there can be a revolution over night. There can just be so much done but I won't do business with a terrorist. I think she's terrorizing a little boy, I really do. She mustn't do that. There's no compromise. There has to be no intimidation of Dan. Dan must have a quiet, stable home life.

In the evenings now, how does it work?

Ingrid comes home, she just says, "Oh my God", before she's even got up the steps. I put things away and she'll come in and say, "When you use the dishcloth, you have to wipe the drops around the sink." I won't do an impression because I'm

81

quite good and I'll make you laugh – and she'll wipe up, because I've left a few drops of water.

Why do you think she's doing that?

It's perfection, it's unattainable so it's always going to be just complete misery, so she'll have to adjust. I mean I can't adjust to perfection. We do have different values. Those things to me are unimportant. When Ingrid says the creases in the curtains aren't right I just think, "Please don't tell me that. There's nothing wrong with not having everything perfect." What's perfection anyway, it's just your interpretation of something isn't it? Her mum was arranging serviettes and they were so perfect, it was frightening.

What's the deeper reason for that?

I don't know, I don't understand the reasons behind what they call it, obsessive compulsive disorder, I don't...

Do you think it's that extreme?

With her mum sometimes, yes, definitely.

So you're saying Ingrid's got to try not to shout and not be so obsessed with perfection. And what in return are you going to... ?

I don't know – anything – just to see her smiling once in a while. Obviously if she comes home and starts to shout and that sets the tone for the rest of the evening.

She seems a very warm person, though.

Yes, that's right... Ingrid is a lovely person, I know that, but at the same time, obviously she has a side with me that other people don't see – and I have probably as well. My friends all think, "What a nice guy," but when I'm with Ingrid, I'm not like that sometimes. We're both nice people, we just don't like each other sometimes. I would say to her, "You won't put me down in that way, I'm a good person. I've got my problems like everyone else, but I'm basically a good person and a good father to Dan." I know she can be an excellent mother but the shouting thing is non-negotiable.

So we've got your wish list of what you'd like from Ingrid – less shouting; less alleged concern with "perfection".

Yes, that's right. It has to work both ways. Sometimes she wakes up in the middle of the night, shouting, "Mum, mum...!" I tell her, "Don't worry, it's all right." It's like terror. Something that happened in the past. She says it's just a nightmare but I worry. When Ingrid read what I said, she felt she had to reply to what I said straight away, pointing a finger in my face, aggressive. It's destroying me. Ingrid says it's all right when Dan hears us arguing, that it doesn't matter. I'd like Gillian and Penny to say it *is* harmful. If she carries on shouting in front of Dan, he will grow up thinking swearing and shouting is how a couple behave. Sometimes I feel I've been selfish. I've put my need to stay because of Dan before his need for peace and quiet...

How about the idea of time doing things for each other?

That's fine. I would also like some time for myself, and Ingrid should have time for herself. I think we're better parents if we do that.

Where do you go?

My friend is the landlord of the pub where we drink, so the door shuts for some but not for others.

You stay there all night?

I admit I've got worse this year. It's an Irish sort of pub. We all stay there late and drink. Ingrid hates it. No women, it's full of Alpha male Irish characters. I slept there one night in a chair in the bar. It was quite bad... but I wouldn't think of doing anything else. I couldn't look myself in the mirror. Ingrid knows that as well. She can trust me. I have left more this year. I realise I'm running away but it's the only way I can communicate. If the screaming stops, loads can happen. She needs therapy or I need therapy. I've no taboos. I need a good kick up the backside sometimes.

So there are lots of arguments in front of Dan?

Ingrid will have to concede on that one. The other day, Dan was in here and she was walking up and down in the hall shouting and screaming. In the end I went out to escape. I went and had a half a pint. But I came back in an hour. Even that was wrong. She said, "You're only coming back so Penny and Gillian will say, 'What a good boy'." I'm saying, "I'm trying to show you I want this to stop." Dan goes to my mum and dad and he sees a different world. On Saturday they took him to the Aquarium on the South Bank. He's normalised there. Normal home life is not about screaming and shouting. If the shouting stops, anything can happen. I really mean that. Anything can happen.

CHAPTER EIGHT
November: Ingrid's second interview

Ingrid and I arranged to meet in Leicester Square and find somewhere quiet to talk. She was a few minutes late. I wondered, briefly, if she had decided to pull out, perhaps alarmed by the lack of control she had over how Tom described her in his interviews.

What had also struck me from our first couple of meetings was how Ingrid, raised by women, had expected to be allowed to rely on Tom's mother as a support and an ally in the ongoing debate about who does what in the house – and to confide in her about their matrimonial problems, even if Tom's mother would then defend her son.

Instead, Tom had forbade Ingrid to speak – and she had obeyed. Thus, ironically, silencing herself when one of her main goals was to persuade the whole family to "open up" about their emotions, especially Tom. So what might persuade Ingrid to break that silence – and with what results?

***

He's so difficult. I prefer to have it all in the open. To know what he's saying and what I'm saying, otherwise how is it going to change? He is so closed. His family are the same. On the surface, it's all open but underneath nobody says anything.

Did you know everything that Tom talked about [in his interview]?

I knew about the suicide... about the pills. I knew he was very sensitive but always something begins after something else happens. He says that once he gets his business going everything is going to be fine [between us as well], "When I get my job this or that will happen." I know he's depressed. *(Ingrid sounds exasperated and looks tearful)*. Sometimes, he behaves as if his mother is the only bright woman in the world. He doesn't see what I do. I tell him, "I'm not your mother. I'm not going to be your mother." He expects me to clean once a week. He leaves his socks on the kitchen table. I say, "Come on! Can't you even do that?"

What did you think about what Gillian and Penny said about both your relationships with your respective parents?

His mother does everything. I asked his mum, "Can Tom clean?" I came home and it was so messy, I was furious. She said "No". Me and Tom had had a big argument and Dan was there. I wanted to make Dan feel okay so I said to Tom's mum, joking, "We should send Tom on a cleaning course," and Dan was laughing.

You get on well with Tom's mother ?

I was surprised when he said I didn't get on well with her. I think she likes me. But when she comes, she never stays. I say, "Would you like a cup of tea?" She never stays. When we talk, it's always about Dan. She never asks me any questions about me or what I do. In Tom's family, everything is fine, fine, fine. No-one discusses their feelings. I want it to be open. They see how different we are and they are trying to protect their son because they have always done things for him. Sometimes I say I'll go to Scandinavia in front of his mother – we can buy a house there, it's cheaper. Tom says, "Oh God, my mother would die if we divorced."

Did you notice Penny and Gillian said that you might both have relationships with your parents that....

My relationship is healthy with my mum. My mum says Tom still does what his parents say.

Dan heard you arguing yesterday?

He was listening to our argument about cleaning. It wasn't yesterday. Tom was washing the dishes. It was just a small thing. I can't stop myself, it's me...

You don't normally lose your temper?

I never lost my temper in my life. The worst time started when Tom stayed home after he left his last job. He wasn't at home for five years so we couldn't argue. If we did argue it was at weekends.

So there has been arguing from the beginning?

Yes. In those years he was always in bed sleeping, always knackered. That's why I couldn't stand him in the house. When I saw him sleeping again [recently] it reminded me. It made me very bitter. When I said, "Why aren't you ever around?", he always used to say, "Tough luck." [The trouble began when] he decided to do the night shift. I said we should discuss it. He said he would. Then later he came home and said he'd done it. He stayed in the job because his best friends were in the job. It was a social life as well. I know that's true. But we [the family] should have been more important.

You had a really hard time with a Caesarian?

I was so ill. I was mentally fine. After five days I came home. But I was taken back twice by ambulance. Over Christmas and New Year. After a month, they opened the scar again because it was infected. The hospital was so dirty I couldn't believe it.

It's interesting that when you came here, you kept your job in Scandinavia open for a year?

I'm not stupid. In case it didn't work out... I wasn't 100 per cent certain.

What made you change your mind and decide to stay?

We had an okay time and then I was pregnant. But Tom's job was a terrible thing in my life. I said to Tom, "Why stay?" His parents were telling him to stay in the job. His father had had the same job in the same place for 40 years. [Tom] wouldn't even take a better job when it was offered.

Why did he leave in the end?

He was waiting for the money [redundancy money] for four years. He was waiting and waiting. It was all good money but look at what the waiting was doing to us.

Are you saying you didn't want him to wait because this

was making you very unhappy?

Yes. Weekends he wanted to go out by himself. He is so immature and I thought, give me a break. At first, I was quite patient. Now, when I see him doing nothing at home or sleeping all the time, it brings it all back. I feel, "Now you have the money and we're still unhappy." I believe in God and I don't think this is right. I rely on my intuition more than Tom does. His mother is very different from me. She won't say to Tom, "Try and do more at home." I understand that she wants to help. She always says that she likes to help because she doesn't have anything else to do. She enjoys it and it helps us [doing the laundry]. But why can't she say to Tom, "You've got to do something as well."

Do you wish that you had talked to your father about what happened?

Yes, I wish I had. I think we were probably very similar.

Why was he in magazines? Was he famous?

I don't know. I would be in a friend's house and sometimes I'd see him in a magazine and I'd quickly turn the pages. I wouldn't say anything.

You saw him in magazines but not in real life?

If he came, I'd go out. I can't remember when we met. When I was a teenager, I didn't want to see him.

Were your previous boyfriends mature or immature?

Mature. They had their own flats, they lived alone. I think they were a good catch, good cars, good jobs, normal childhoods. The first lived in my town. He had money but his past. He was adopted as a baby. I think my intuition told me [to stay away]. When I left he took it in a hard way...

Do you think you can sort out your relationship with Tom?

Something has to change. Quite a lot. But how can we change our personalities?

Have you tried what Gillian and Penny suggested – being more positive towards each other ?

I know I have to do something but I'm so bitter. He hasn't said, "I'm sorry, I shouldn't have spent those years doing nights."

Is that what would you like him to say?

He made a big mistake. He got the money but now it's all gone. I have a psychology book that says, "If you do good, you get it back." Tom doesn't seem to understand that. He can't get into his head.

If he said, "Ingrid, it was a big mistake, I'm really sorry..."

It would help a lot. I'd stop nagging. He never said, "okay, I made a mistake." Obviously, he's worried about money and bills and everyday life but, when I do something, I trust my instinct. I feel it's right. His view is that of a young boy. He says to himself, I made my money. I have my goal. He doesn't weigh up the consequences [of his choices]. Sometimes he says that I'm the baby. But he never understands the "Why?". What Penny and Gillian said about the "Why?" was good. It's the "Why?" [we do something] that matters. My English sometimes gets in the way. Also, his mother never complains and does everything. Someone has to tell him that's not how women today behave.

Someone has to tell him? You want Gillian and Penny to tell him it isn't normal for a woman to do it all?

Yes. In Scandinavia, a lot of men help. My sister's husband

does a lot. Many times now, Tom takes Dan out to places I'd like to go but I stay cleaning even when it's sunny.

Why does it matter if it gets dirty?

But this is dirty, dirty. It takes me two hours on a Thursday night, but five hours if it gets really dirty. That's too much to do.

Are you going to do something together this weekend? That's what Gillian and Penny suggested?

I suppose so. We can laugh about it. We don't argue all the time. We haven't been to Scandinavia for one Christmas in seven years. Now Tom says we should all go, but the business hasn't started. It's already November and next month is Christmas. We have to decide soon but money will be tight. Sometimes I think Tom dreams too much.

Would you like to go?

Maybe not. Too many things in my head. I want to get the relationship straight. Perhaps my mother should come here.

Will it be okay if you're not getting on well?

We're okay with other people around. We're not just "aaargh!" all the time. My mum was here two years ago and we started to argue. She understood me because she knows me. She tried to explain to Tom how I felt, doing so much – I translated. But she also tells me not to worry about stupid little things. I told her they are not stupid little things. They mean something. *(Looks upset)* This business is in my head all the time. If the other guy (Tom's business partner) says it's not going to work, I don't know what will happen. This has already happened once before. Over three years ago. Tom was really excited but then the other guy pulled out. And another time, the guy took all the money. Tom has been so unlucky.

Does Tom know how you feel? Are you concerned that he can't manage?

Three years ago, he was so babyish it could never work. He just thought, "I'm going to get rich." Now, he has the estate agent qualifications. He has done the homework and he should get somewhere now. He's too honest sometimes.

What happens if the business doesn't work?

He could get a job. He has qood qualifications. Sometimes, when he's drunk, he opens up and I do listen... But why does he have to be drunk? Gillian and Penny said he should think more about his own drinking than mine... I'm not stupid. My father was an alcoholic. And I am health-conscious. But... Tom told you about Saturday? I felt so terrible. I had detoxed and not eaten for ten days and not drunk much. Then I came out of the restaurant... the bus door shut [hit Ingrid's head] and I felt so stupid. I rang Tom.

He sounds as if he was concerned about you...

I know. We're waiting for something to happen. It's a small flat. We want to live somewhere nice. We're waiting, waiting. For the money, for the business. I knew it wasn't going to be easy. We're stuck in the situation. We need something to happen. To wake us both up. Sometimes I don't believe anything will change. Perhaps one day he'll lose everything and Tom will realise what really matters. Maybe that would be a good thing.

You decided it was a good idea to read what Tom had said [in the transcript of the interview sent by e-mail]?

It was good in the end, I know. But I won't read his e-mails again.

So will you do what Gillian and Penny have suggested?

I know we have to do something.

CHAPTER NINE

December: Penny and Gillian's second response

Gillian and Penny both said it must have been very diffi-cult for Tom to have had his interview read by Ingrid. One immediate result was that the proposal that they should each try and do something positive for the other had become sidelined. But it was still important to try.

Before we continued the discussion, I told them that I couldn't understand why both Tom and Ingrid were each holding so tightly to a particular issue even when, by doing so, they were further damaging their relationship. Ingrid wouldn't let go of Tom's years on nights. Tom was adamant that Ingrid's shouting was the cause of many of their prob-lems. Ingrid wants Tom to apologise sincerely for those first several years when he was never around. Tom wants Ingrid to stop getting so angry. They both imply that, if each makes that concession, the real process of change begin – except that, depressingly, neither Tom nor Ingrid give any indication that they themselves are prepared to budge.

Four months into the process, are we already at stalemate? Gillian and Penny suggested that it might be worthwhile to look at why "no change", at this stage, looks like an attractive strategy to both Ingrid and Tom – no matter how destructive.

***

Tom and Ingrid may both be reluctant to begin the process of rebuilding the relationship because of ambivalence (one or both of them really doesn't want to revive the marriage). Or it may be due to fear (what if the process fails?) or the fact that holding onto the anger – in the way that each is doing in different ways – has become more important than creating something fresh. Or perhaps, it's a mixture of all these reasons. Both Tom and Ingrid convey the impression that they each long to be looked after – and both are furious because neither has the capacity to look after the other, in the way that each desires.

Tom and Ingrid are also, perhaps, handicapped by the absence of a model of what a long-term relationship based on equality involves. A sense of reality is required about how a relationship changes and adapts over a period of years. In many relationships, eventually one or both partners looks at the other – and seriously questions whether this is the man or woman with whom they dreamed of spending the rest of their lives.

They might ask, "If I were to start again, would I pick this man/woman?" Sometimes, that questioning results in separation. Sometimes, it encourages a man and woman to seek out the positive (if changed and different) aspects of the other person, and to look again at what they have built between them in the relationship, and value it. In this way, the focus of both individuals may be shifted from the minus ("He doesn't do this... she doesn't do that...") to the plus ("He may not be the man I thought he was but six years into the marriage, I've changed too...")

Finding accommodation with each other as you are *now* is perhaps more constructive than constantly referring back. Negativity itself can become a very destructive habit. It also prevents a couple from developing an idea of what their relationship might be. And telling each other the story of why they value each other and what they have created together. Of course, some conflict can be constructive, if it encourages two individuals to adjust to each other's changing needs.

It is known from extensive research that a woman shouting pushes a man away. It's not *what* it is being said – but *how* it is being said that alienates the man. He doesn't get beyond the yelling; so shouting becomes counter-productive, if the aim is for the woman to have her grievances heard and acknowledged. In one study, once the women learned to control their rage better, the men began to understand more about why the women were angry in the first place.

Tom says he left home recently after an argument but returned within a relatively short time – a break from his previous pattern of behaviour, disappearing for hours, occasionally an entire night. If possible, Ingrid might value this sign of change and tell Tom so, rather than treat it in a negative fashion.

Tom, too, might try to place himself in Ingrid's shoes. Perhaps her allegedly obsessional standards of cleanliness and order in the house isn't just to do with tidiness and who does what domestically. We are suggesting a more complex motivation. This is partly to do with control; and partly a means of "punishing" Tom (another way of saying, "You're not good enough.") Since Tom has been home all the time, if might be that Ingrid is no longer at ease in her own house. She feels displaced, like a domestic refugee. Tom is there all the time, so how can she leave her own mark? The housework is a subconscious way of reclaiming "her" territory – although it means she pays the biggest price, losing family time with her son to carry out domestic duties, as she says.

The main reason to remove the block between Ingrid and Tom is the welfare of their son, Dan. There is now a large amount of research that tells us that no matter how outwardly sociable and at ease a child may be – conflict between his or her parents, witnessing constant arguments, can have a deeply detrimental effect. It has an effect in several key ways. It's obviously distressing for the child to see. The child doesn't care who is right or wrong – he is upset to see the people he loves most so miserable. He may blame himself. Outwardly, he may look "happy" but that may mean his worries have been internalised.

If dad treats mother with contempt, the child reasons, soon he will treat me like that. If mum is frightened, this damages the child's sense of security. A mother and father in recurring conflict have their parenting skills impaired because, however hard they may try, they are distracted by their own preoccupations and hostilities. In one study, a nine-year-old described how he felt when his parents argued. He said, "When my mum and dad argue it's not like they are my mum and dad. They are like two different people."

We strongly suggest that Ingrid and Tom should try and place themselves in Dan's shoes. It must be a frightening experience to witness his parents at war; to see two "strangers" in his family on a regular basis. He hears one or the other threatening to leave – how would Ingrid and Tom feel if they were a six-year-old, hearing that they might "lose" a parent?

The reliance on Tom's mother, is also perhaps having an impact on Tom and Ingrid's ability to take responsibility themselves for making change, and improving circumstances for themselves and Dan.

Both Ingrid and Tom might consider what would happen if Tom's parents were unable to take Dan for regular days out or for overnights? How would they create a happy home environment for their son, left to their own devices? However much Dan loves his grandparents, most children want a reasonable enough home life with their mum and dad. Might Ingrid and Tom consider removing the block between them – no matter who is right or wrong – because one of their goals is for their son to live peacefully with both parents? The potential for change in their relationship is still strong – still, acknowledging the need for it is far easier than the next step – making it happen.

CHAPTER TEN
Children

One of the enduring images I have of my childhood is of a lone suitcase parked at the front door. Several different front doors in fact because as a family we moved often. The suitcase belonged to my mother and it signalled that there had been yet another row – but, this time, it had gone too far. My mother was going to take herself and me, an only child, off to somewhere else. The family was about to splinter. The miracle is that we never actually left.

My parents, as many do, argued furiously for years and years and a certain level of anxiety became a "normal" part of my family life. How, as a child, could I make it better? The rows would be interspersed with days of frozen silence broken only by my mother or father asking me to act as messenger, ensuring that the continuity of the domestic routine was maintained. "Ask your father if he wants chops for supper." "Tell your mother I'm taking the car in for a service." I guess, on reflection, my parents could be categorised as a "high con-

99

flict" couple. They also, at other times, had a life together and apart that they enjoyed. They lived abroad for much of the time; they were gregarious and they were good at entertaining and being entertained. I, too, had all the usual distractions of childhood – school, friends, the freedom to roam in a way that isn't so common now. But sometimes there was no escaping the fights.

On occasions, they literally forgot themselves and let rip in front of me. That was frightening but not nearly as scary as listening to an intermittent sound-track of anger and contempt through a bedroom wall. What if they killed each other? What would happen to me? At the time, of course, you believe you are the only child living on the edge of a precipice. And you are to blame.

Did I wish they had separated? As a teenager, definitely, yes. If nothing else, to give us all respite. But, at that age, you know only a fraction of the story. After 60 years, they are still together. The truce they brokered twenty years ago, partly as a result of exhaustion, moved into a kind of contentment rooted in shared experiences, surviving crises and interlocking values, and a belief that they were in this together facing a world that wasn't as good as it once was.

"I know your father," my mother would say. "She thinks she does," my dad would add before Alzheimer's took hold. But it was spoken in peace. Each of my parents had forfeited something very precious to them but, in doing so, they also recognised a mutual need. My dad, in particular, didn't know how to live with my mother and she wasn't about to make many concessions – but he also instinctively knew he would somehow be less of a man without her.

The first time I met Dan, it reminded me of how my family might have appeared to an outsider. My parents, in the company of others, were warm, funny, hospitable and everything looked fine – just as Tom and Ingrid appear. Then, in private, the rows would erupt and, as with Tom and Ingrid's conflicts, very little was resolved. As Dan grows older what will seem ever more baffling is that, days later, exactly the same argument begins again. He may come the fear that, somehow, it's all his fault.

Although, children are told they are not to blame – there's a grain of truth in the view. Children obviously do have a huge impact on a relationship. Couples who believe a baby will bring them closer together labour under an illusion. Most research suggests that couples become less satisfied with their relationship once they become parents. Child-free marriages report much higher and consistent levels of contentment – and this is especially true for women.

In one study, only 38 per cent of women with infants had higher than average marital satisfaction, compared with 62 per cent of childless women. The presence of children has even more of a negative effect on marital satisfaction among the higher socio-economic groups. Women in professional jobs, working full-time may experience the conflict in their roles especially harshly – and the restriction to their freedom once babies arrive.

Studies suggest that, more than ever before, there is an even greater contrast between the lifestyles of young, childless adults and parents with young children. This gap is accentuated by advertising that portrays child-free people living a life of high-octane pleasure and unmitigated excitement and glamour. How alienated does that make a cash-strapped, sleep-deprived couple feel, caring for a two-month-old with colic?

The decision to have a child may itself cause a split. It implies, in theory at least, staying together for life and that can prompt a man or woman to question whether they want to remain with the other partner. The arrival of the baby also obviously changes the focus in a relationship. At the same time, the father is often pushed into the wings by professionals surrounding the birth – health visitors, midwives – while the pressure to continue earning a wage means that his time with the child is rationed. Ten to fifteen per cent of mothers suffer from post-natal depression, but it was only in 2005 that research revealed that some fathers also experience post-natal depression.

In a paper published in *The Lancet*, Paul Amchandani and colleagues, including members from the Avon Longitudinal Study of Parents and Children, established that paternal "post-natal depression has a specific and detrimental effect on children's early behavioural and emotional development." Research by Professor Charlie Lewis of Lancaster University indicates that the most dissatisfied men are those working full time who are also trying to be involved fathers. As a result, in some families, while the mother feels overloaded, the father may take flight, out of despair because he either doesn't know how to offer support when paid work is so demanding, or because he believes himself unable to make a difference.

Some mothers can become hugely possessive and territorial when the baby arrives. "He's useless" may be reinterpreted as, "He's useless – because I give him little alternative." Many women exercise control in the domestic sphere in a way that makes it difficult for fathers "to do anything right." Alternatively, some men do so little that partners retaliate by criticising their contribution, however small, and so conflict builds up. Some fathers, especially if they are out of the home for long periods of time, underestimate not just the the time and effort tiny babies require – but also the huge psychological adjustment some women have to make; relinquishing the control they once had over their time, ambitions and the view they had of themselves.

There are couples who manage to navigate these tricky waters well. Stress in a relationship is obviously reduced if two people can talk about how they are going to handle the adjustments – and appreciate each other's contributions. Conflict itself is a signal that one or both people in a relationship feel unsupported. A long-term view also helps. However tough it is in the first couple of years, babies grow older – and children do bring enormous rewards that are often all the better for being shared.

Many adults, according to surveys, believe that their sons and daughters are somehow impervious to rows between grown-ups. In one study, seven out of ten teenagers rated parents getting on well together as an important factor in raising children. In contrast, only a third of parents thought this was an important issue. In truth, even very young children notice when the matrimonial temperature drops from luke warm to icy cold. Research published in 2005 by American psychologist Professor John Gottman, author of *Making Marriage Work*, indicates that babies born into marriages rated as "troubled", tended to cry and fuss more. The happier the father with his partner, the more engaged he was with his child. Fathers who were judged unhappily married tended to withdraw or over-stimulate their babies, so the child became difficult to soothe. "It isn't so much a matter of staying married for the sake of the kids," Professor Gottmam says. "Couples need to stay happily married, if they can, in order to help their children."

In their research review, "Not in Front of the Children?", the relationship organisation One Plus One explains that children do not get used to discord. They become more sensitive to it and more vulnerable to its effects. Warring, unhappy partners are distracted parents. Preoccupied with their own feelings and less attuned to their children's needs, their parenting tends to become inconsistent and ineffective.

However, in an "empty" adult relationship with minimal rows, children can thrive so long as their parents continue to show interest and affection. The young can also weather arguments so long as they witness two grown-ups "making up". Understanding how difficulties can be resolved is a valuable lesson for children to learn.

What is not good is a high degree of adult conflict that is constant and open-ended. Tragically, conflict that begins in a relationship often continues during and after divorce. An American study of 56 teenagers revealed that children from divorced high-conflict families did less well academically and socially than children in high-conflict intact families where parents had expressed thoughts of divorce.

In another, fifteen-year American study, tracking more than 2000 married people, conducted by Paul Amato and Alan Booth, children experienced their parents' divorce in a high conflict marriage as a relief. But when marriages that were "good enough" from the children's point of view were ended, they saw it as inexplicable and extremely painful. Amato and Booth said that only a third of divorces ended high-conflict marriages, leading one to assume that the other two-thirds may have been "fixable" but the couples were unable or unwilling to make the effort. Or perhaps one or both parties had been seduced by the idea that happiness is a "right" in adult life and is not gleaned from a relationship that requires work. Amato and Booth made the following suggestion: "Spending a third of one's life living in a marriage that is less than satisfactory in order to benefit children – children whom parents elected to bring into the world – is not an unreasonable expectation." Especially since, as they point out, "Many people who divorce and remarry find that their second marriage is no happier than their first."

From a child's point of view, new partners bring a whole new set of problems: step-parents, the difficulty of living in two households with different sets of rules, the arrival of a new baby in one or both of their parents' new families and the possible accompanying feeling that he or she is now the unwanted cuckoo in two nests. Many "reconstituted" families manage the business well. For those who don't, children tend to exit the family in their teens, when the need for love and support is nonetheless still vitally important.

In *The Case for Marriage*, Waite and Gallagher argue that "bad" marriages can be turned around. According to an analysis of the American National Survey of Families and Households by Waite, 86 per cent of unhappily married couples who stick it out, found that five years later, their marriages were "happier". Seventy-seven per cent who rated their marriage as very unhappy five years later said that the relationship was "very happy or "quite happy". Only fifteen per cent of those who initially said they were unhappily married (and who stayed married) continued to say their marriages were very unhappy. For the others, something radical appears to have shifted. The hope is that, as a result, it's the children who may have reaped the most benefit.

Chapter Eleven

December: Tom's third interview

Again, we met in the same hotel. Earlier in the week, I had received several e-mails from Tom that made it sound as if a real change was underway. Little did I realise that this was the beginning of a much-repeated, soft shoe shuffle that involved three steps forward, and three or even four steps back. At this meeting, Tom appeared much more optimistic. He said he and Ingrid had exchanged e-mails and lain down some rules to improve their relationship.

***

TOM: The upshot was that Ingrid said basically, "I'm never going to shout in front of Dan again." So, I was over the moon. Oh my God, a big weight lifted and stop with all this, "Five years rubbish... the last five years..." Can we just stop with that? Can we just agree that, whatever the reasons, it went wrong and I'm not saying it's my fault, I've got my reasons you've got yours. That was about a week or two ago. There's definitely been a big improvement in front of Dan, a big improvement. I said to you that I would love Gillian and Penny to mention something about that. She's definitely mellowed a little bit since reading that. Whether it's just because she's having a lull, I don't know. I think it's too early to say, the cycle hasn't gone through yet, so I don't know.

Do you think you've actually changed as well?

Yes, maybe I'm just watching Ingrid and waiting for the next thing to go wrong sometimes, or hoping it doesn't. I think the more it goes on, and it's better, the more positive things will happen but the fact that this has been done is an achievement. It's just us agreeing to disagree – not agreeing to disagee, agreeing to move on perhaps...

What happened last weekend? What did you do? Did you go to football?

I'd been out probably once. I was out all night but I phoned Ingrid. I came home totally sober. Basically that was the only time I've done that.

Why is that?

Because I think I've probably been self-indulgent with my behaviour and, even though I had a perfect excuse, it's now time to look at myself a bit and think, well, if I carry on, then all the good work's that been done is not going to mean anything is it? The only thing now is, I will now have to be working seven days a week till it [the business] gets going. I mean Jack [the new employer] has a work ethic. He works seven days a week and he's making an absolute packet. He's a multi-millionaire. I'm not just an employee of his business, I'm on

25 per cent of the profits and if this works, then I've said to Ingrid, as soon as we can afford it, finish your work a couple of hours earlier every day.

So you've been negotiating?

That's the first thing the money should do is alleviate some of her pressures so it makes it easier.

That's fantastic because you're now talking to each other about the future?

Don't even go there *(laughs)*, but I think Ingrid has definitely mellowed. False dawns and things like that, it's been seven years. I said to you, if she stops shouting, anything can happen. I really mean that but I'm working ridiculously long hours again, Ingrid, sorry about that...

Can you see the difference though between how Ingrid sees long hours now and the nights you worked in your last job?

Of course, it's different because in this one... I've got a chance. if I don't make a seriously huge amount of money in a few year's time doing this, then I'm an arsehole and I need a kick up the backside quite frankly.

Did you recognise what Gillian and Penny said, that it might not just be about cleanliness?

Yes, of course, I've always thought that Ingrid was just angry, and that's anger manifesting itself through the most unlikely vehicles, I know. Obviously she's pissed off and frustrated but at the same time, one is causing the other. I did have a revelation the other night. Basically I've always thought, since this process started, that it was me who had the baggage, me who had the problems, me who had everything, and I just think now Ingrid's suffered much more than me. I still think

Ingrid's learning to cope with her father. I've gone through my hurt process and changed and Ingrid maybe hasn't. She's never really come to terms with her father and I just think that's so sad.

Did you say that to her?

No, I wanted to say it to you. I don't think we're at the stage where I can talk like that to her. That would just be throwing dynamite onto a fire if I did that. But I think it's something you or Gillian and Penny would consider.

One of the things they [Gillian and Penny] asked me to do was to get you to ask yourself, on the subject of your leaving, what that would lead to? Realistically, you don't have much money. Would you go back home?

No, are you joking? No, that's the last place I ever want to go. I think there's a theme[(from Gillian and Penny] about my mum doing the washing and all that sort of stuff, which I think is so funny because it's only been the last six months or so that she's ever done anything like that, and it only started because Ingrid was sort of saying, hinting to my mum that Tom never does this and my mum said, "Let me help Ingrid out."

So you don't think you're over-engaged with your parents? It is interesting that your sister's gone to South Africa which is about as far away as you can get

Oh right, you think tha *(laughs)* My father and sister don't get on. Well, they do get on but I always think, yes, he's slightly pissed off. Kate is extremely boisterous. She disappeared for a few years and went to South Africa and came back a slightly different person.

Is it that, or is it that she's become more of an independent woman?

Oh, fair play to her, I've got a lot of respect for what she's done. I mean I get on better with Kate than any of the rest of my family – apart from my mum. I think they tolerate her to some degree. She's extremely domineering, she tramples over her lovely husband. I just love Bill, he's just a lovely guy, there's not a bad bone in the guy's body. But Kate... I just think they've got their roles, one's submissive and one's certainly not. Kate's very tough. If she is tough and loud and stroppy and the rest of it, she needed to be...

...Tough women don't go down well?

Well, with me they don't. Although I married one and I've got a sister for one, so I can't be a hypocrite can I? *(laughs)*

What about Dan? Has he noticed any difference ?

Dan won the headmaster's award and I went to see him get it in front of the whole school: I'm just so pleased and proud of him... I'm so happy that he's doing so well.

What about the idea of doing something for each other?

Well, we've been out with my brother and his wife, we've been out to two [Christmas] parties, not too bad at all, we didn't have one screaming match, that was really good, even though Ingrid was pissed once... well, all the time, each time, she was pissed, but there was no screaming matc We went to dinner and had a really nice evening and there was loads of drinking going on, and it was just a good laugh.

So when you came back from the evenings out, you just peaceably went to bed.

I did get annoyed. We went to the West End and it's a £35

cab. I said to Ingrid, "You get the black cab and I'll pay for it. I was mucking about, it didn't go down very well. She said, "Don't say stupid things, it doesn't matter who pays," or something like that and it got more out of proportion to what it should have been. I couldn't care less. Honestly, I've always paid for everything. I can accept that, even though sometimes it does piss me off, I've learnt to accept it.

Why?…

Well, I've had to learn to accept it because I think it doesn't suit the fact that she wants to be an independent modern woman and, at the same time, she behaves in traditional ways. For me, it's having your cake and eating it as well, isn't it?

Have you spoken to her about it?

I don't because. I don't really get any respect from her when I talk about it, so I don't bother.

From what you were saying, it's not about money, it's the principle. But I'm interested: why you can't have this conversation with Ingrid? It's almost as if you have a conversation with each other via Penny and Gillian.

That's right, yes. That's what we have needed to do because we can't sit down and have a discussion like we're having now. It's not possible, we need mediators.

But money clearly does niggle you.

Yes, it really does niggle me, if the truth be known. Well, it niggles me but I've had to swallow it and repress it. If you are really this independent, striving, contemporary young thing that you think you are, then don't let a bloke dominate you by letting him pay for everything forever. I've never known Ingrid to walk into a bar and say, "What do you want to drink?" – ever, ever. I walk into a bar with Ingrid's friends and they all stand round the bar and I'm the one who has to walk over [and buy the round]. I just mentioned about the taxi and I said I had to go to a cash-point, and she started screaming, "Don't tell everyone you have to go to a cash-point, they'll think we're poor", or something like that. I just couldn't believe it. I said, "The Queen has to go to the cash-point, so what are you talking about?"

Is Ingrid paying the rent?

No, she gives me £500 a month.

And how much is the rent?

It's £800. We've got a couple of loans as well, for £200/£300 and things like that and that's all included in that. Plus I pay gas, electric, phone; she pays council tax. It's split down the middle. She's on twenty grand a year now, it's not great money but she doesn't pay tax, so she can afford to do that.

So you're saying what you really want is gestures; it's not so much just the amount of money?

Let's put it this way, we've been out three times, okay. That's £90 in taxis that I've paid in the last three days, and that's not including drinks, clubs or anything else. What respect do you give to someone who just takes. It's not a case of "Thanks for paying the taxi", it's a case of, you know, "You're the man".

So if Ingrid occasionally said, "Let me buy a drink", or "Let me pay for a taxi," that's what you'd like?

I'd like that.

Do you buy each other flowers or anything?

No, Ingrid's never bought… For Christmas last year, I bought a pair of diamond earrings and she said, "They're not very big, are they?" Bloody cheek, about £800-worth.

Did she really say that?

She wasn't as callous as that. I'm just making the situation worse by saying that.

Did she really say that?

I can't remember. She really liked them but I think we were having such a bad time, I just went and bought them because I should do. That's just the wrong reason. There was no affection attached to it, which is totally wrong. But I knew that I had to buy something that she would attach affection to, otherwise it was going to make it worse. It was like playing a game, to be honest. If you ask a psychologist what's attached to a diamond, it's a deep, meaningful gesture – but for me, it wasn't.

So what are your reasons for staying together?

I've got to say my motivation is… this whole thing is Dan. My main aim is to normalise Dan's upbringing. If it means that I'm unhappy for the rest of my life, that's what it will take. Otherwise, I couldn't care less in some respects which is really bad. But it means that I will obviously do what it takes to put Dan first in everything.

But if you say you're prepared to be unhappy… to normalise Dan's life, that's a contradiction in terms.

Of course it is. It's not his fault he was born, it was mine and Ingrid's, it was our action, so we are responsible for getting him to the stage where he can initiate his own life.

Gillian and Penny are trying to say that you have to tell yourself a story about the positive side of your relationship with

Ingrid. There must have been something about her because you were very determined at first, you weren't going to let her go.

No, that's right. I must admit I don't give up on anything. I'm very, very tough in some respects.

When Ingrid talks about you, she has enormous confidence in you. Whatever she may say that sounds critical, she may be trying to make you think, focus your thoughts.

Good, that's nice. I've got enormous confidence in my own ability to do things but I'm tired of getting it wrong or nearly always getting it wrong for Ingrid, I don't know. I bought flowers, I thought they were really beautiful. She said, "Bloody hell, don't you know. Red is love and yellow is friendship?"

And what had you bought her?

Yellow. What a laugh, I couldn't believe it. I didn't know there was a colour code for flowers… very funny.

What do you think Ingrid was trying to say to you? There must be lots of good things that you could see in her.

Yeah, definitely. I fell for Ingrid because she had a very open, expressive face and is very honest about the way she said things.

That's exactly what you're now saying is the problem.

It is a problem obviously about how things come out, because it's not processed. About the cash-point, when she said people will think we're poor. When we eventually got inside and I said, "What the hell are you doing, Ingrid?" Then, it's arms around me and "I'm sorry…" Why does she have to shout in front of everyone? What was that about?

She shouts at you in public?

Yes, she screams. (*Mimics Ingrid's voice*) "TOM!" – I hate indiscretion like that, I cannot have it. I mean if you want to say something to me, come up to me, whisper in my ear discreetly, and I have no problem with it, but don't shout across the road. I would never dream of doing it to her. If I was to shout at her in public like that, people would say, "My god, look how he treats his wife." If it's a male who shouts at a woman, it's: "Look at that poor suffering housewife, that bullying bastard."

Fresh things are now coming up... the money thing and what you see as Ingrid's coldness and her insensitivity sometimes. You've also said that Ingrid's attraction was that she could be honest and open and generous; she does seem like a generous person.

Certainly in her opinion *(laughs)*. But Ingrid is repressed about things. Whereas I don't think there's such a thing as a taboo subject.

Have you talked to her then about her father and her childhood?

Oh yeah, but she doesn't really remember her father. When he died, she was very sad, so that said everything. It means that you are now realising that your father was incredibly important, and she's only got her mum's side of how he was. She was brought up in an extremely female-dominated environment. Sometimes I doubt her ability to be a good mother. She doesn't know how to communicate with Dan. I tell her, Dan didn't come with a rule book. If you want him to do something, you have to explain why. Instead, she just shouts louder... I'm tired of Ingrid crying, and me getting pissed or her having a drink... Nobody wants to admit they are in trouble but our need for a mediator becomes more essential as we go along...

How do you think Christmas will be?

Honestly, I want Ingrid and Dan to have a really nice Christmas. I really want to make Christmas a family thing... a happy time. I hope.

CHAPTER TWELVE

December: Ingrid's third interview

At this meeting, Ingrid appeared much calmer, though perhaps more resigned than optimistic. As if the day-to-day routine had improved but not the core issues in the marriage. I was beginning to worry that improvement, if it happened at all, would take a very, very long time – longer than we had. And, even more disturbing, where would that leave the couple at the end of twelve months?

***

Do you think things have changed?
I don't know if they've changed. Obviously Tom doesn't go out so much but... Or, when he does go out, he comes back. He's not out all night as much. The last couple of weeks have been okay. I asked him to come to an [office] party. I said "Let's forget about things and have a nice time." I didn't mean forget about all our problems for the past seven years. Okay,

it's stupid to shout in front of Dan. I raised my voice last night as well a little bit but I can't say anything without Tom saying I'm shouting. He shouts too. He said sorry and things by email but he never says those things in person...

Is that an improvement or not?

It might be; it's good he says those things because I often said he is like his family, he keeps things to himself, he should be more open. He should talk more. Sometimes, I don't recognise myself, when I read what I've said. I can't always express myself well.

Apparently it has got much calmer?

For a couple of weeks I have tried not to shout so much, not to say anything. It's not so difficult because the good thing is he's started his business and he's changed.

Has he?

He's changed because he is more positive but he's stopped doing anything at home and I do so much. He doesn't do anything else in the house, housework or anything. Work is very important for him, but I don't mind so much doing housework if I can see he's working. He works seven days.

Do you mind about him having to work seven days?

No, I don't mind if it's good for the business. I didn't expect anything else. I did mind when he was working in his previous bloody job and...

So are you saying that it's okay to work long hours if you think it's going to create more opportunities for the family?

And he's happy now and he wasn't happy [then], he was complaining all the time. There have been so many times when he went into business and it didn't work out.

119

You must be doing something, because you're the one that raises her voice and you're clearly not doing that any more.

Yes, but he really shouts as well. It's not just me shouting, do you understand? It's up to me to organise everything. Shopping, cleaning, Dan. I said to Tom why don't you do a little bit, put those clothes away – you don't have to clean. I'm not obsessive like he says. No, it's just normal things.

They [Penny and Gillian] are saying it's not just about cleaning, it's about feeling that everything is getting out of control.

I don't care who cleans. It's just that, if I'm cleaning I can't spend time with Dan and that's not fair. Tom doesn't understand that. We talked about that last night.

Did it resolve itself before it became a big row?

I did raise my voice but not like before. I was cross. He came home late because I came back late the other night as well. I came home at 9.30.

And was he okay about that?

He was, in the end. He wouldn't speak to me and I said, "Okay, sorry".

If you're saying sorry and he's saying okay, that's a big change. Does Tom stay out overnight now?

He hasn't done it as much, only once. Tom went out on Saturday and he didn't come back. I woke up at six am and he wasn't home. I think it's important that he informs me if he's not coming home because I was worried.

Did he phone you?

In the morning, yes, at 8am I got a message.

So he didn't tell you that he wouldn't be home?

I tried to call him but he didn't reply.

That must be horrible – not knowing where he is? When he did come home, did you have an argument?

No.

You didn't say to him, "Why didn't you call?"

No, I said go to bed and then we'll go out with Dan... I was being okay. But, if he goes every weekend, then I'd be annoyed.

Do you think money is an issue between you? Do you share the bills?

Yeah, I pay for a lot of things, I think I pay more than he does in the end because he pays gas and electricity, but I pay council tax, £120 every month.

So why do you think this money thing has come up?

I don't know. Yeah, he paid all the taxis. but we haven't been out for such a long time, so...

Maybe it's not about the money, maybe it's about something else. One of the things that Penny and Gillian said is that anger damages the person who displays the anger more than anyone else. They said, when you start to feel angry, which is understandable, you should walk away, literally, physically walk away or think through it: ie. if I show my anger, what will happen then? I know it's really hard when you're feeling angry.

Yes, but he never talks about things, how can I just walk away? I did that for five years and we ended up never speaking. We never took the time to sit down and talk. Tom wants to keep it all inside.

Tom told me Dan had a school prize?

Yes, he did very well. He's very bright and he's very good. I know it's not fair for him. I think sometimes the problem is that Tom has never lived alone, that's one thing. He has always had someone to look after him, to pick up his clothes, do his washing. Tom says that I can't cook or stuff – he's just saying those things, to be cruel. His whole family is sometimes aggressive

Verbally aggressive?

Yes, they are.

Do you each have the same idea about Dan, about what time he goes to bed, or, for instance, what he should eat?

Yes, I put Dan to bed every night and… every other night, I say, to Tom, "Okay can you do it." Like yesterday, I was so knackered and, okay, I know I came in late the other night but it's not like that every night. I've told Tom, "It's time you did the things that you've never done; Dan's lunch box and cooking and putting him to bed."

How much of how you are feeling is to do with Tom and how much of that is to do with Dan?

How do you mean?

Having a child does take up your time, even if you've got the perfect marriage?

That's right. I think it's my own thing as well, about doing everything. If Tom washes up, I think it isn't good enough but I don't say so.

If Tom's in charge, then you have to let him have his standards, and when you're in charge, you have your standards. Perhaps there's another issue, it's not just to do with you and Tom, it's to do with the way that Dan impinges on your time; children take up a lot of time.

Yes, they do, that's right and I don't mind but perhaps it's something to do with my childhood? Every night I wash Dan's clothes. Tom doesn't do that, I make his lunch box. Okay, Tom does take him to school but I do everything else. I buy his clothes, I look after what he's wearing, I take him out, things Tom doesn't even think about.

This morning you were arguing?

It was just a stupid argument. I put the washing machine on [last night]. I was really knackered. And, when I woke up in the morning, he had left everything in the machine. I was so angry when I woke up: "How could you do this?"

Supposing you waited until later and you said, when you were calmer, "Tom, the thing about leaving wet clothes is... they don't dry."

I've said many times.

Is Tom the kind of man you expected to marry?

He was in many ways but our past is so different. There is a cultural thing, too. Sometimes I see many good things about him and I would still marry him but culture does matter. My sister's husband is so different. He helps with the children, he cleans everything up at home. I'm not saying their marriage is perfect, they have had problems, but in Scandinavia the men are used to doing more.

What about doing what Gillian and Penny were suggesting – try and forget a lot of what has happened in the previous years and just say, "How are we going to make it work from now on?"

It's not that easy. Tom's a grown-up but he doesn't behave like one sometimes. He can be obsessive, so it annoys me when people think I am the only one who is angry. You hear one side – the problem is not just my shouting, Tom loses his temper more than I do. He throws things, he throws things in front of Dan. I worry sometimes that it may be something in his [Tom's] head ? Oh my God, he's so angry, he is bad.

In front of Dan?

Yes, maybe I say something about the cleaning and then… I try to say something and he tells me to shut up.

He says he's talking about you and you automatically assume something negative.

That may be true but he never calls me, I always call him "How are you? What are you doing?" He will say, "Why are you calling me?" I call him, I always call him; he doesn't call me.

Do you see a future together? What would make things different now?

I would like to have more time. I leave early and come home late, so how can I do anything? I'm not even worried about Tom, I'm worried about me and Dan because I don't have time. Even on a weekend, normally Tom goes [out with Dan] and I clean.

What if you didn't clean?

Our house is so untidy. If you could see it now, you would say, "Oh, my god. Tom just leaves everything anywhere."

How are you going to see Tom in a more positive light? I know that may be really hard…

Yes, we can't go back. We have to sort it out. In the end, I know he loves me. I think it's something to do with his past. Obviously, I had my past but I was very secure.

I've met you three times and each time, at the end, when we finished recording, you've said you think this is something to do with your father? Gillian and Penny suggested looking at not who your father might have been as a person, but what it might mean to you not to have had a father? Does your sister talk to you about him?

She says she remembers feeling really left out. She was older so she grieved when he died. I never felt like that. She needed to be an adult and she had a lot of clashes with my mother. She had to do everything. I felt guilty because I had friends and she was really rebellious. I never smoked. I never had really bad problems.

In comparison to Tom?

You mean with the pills and depression?

Have you talked to him about that now?

He doesn't want to talk about it. Obviously, I say we should, because it is something affecting our relationship because of the way his girlfriend treated him. He always says to me, "I'm not going to have sex with you." He's the one who says no. I think something happened really badly with his girlfriend.

Do you think he's punishing you for what she did?

Yes, maybe. I think he decided to do nights because... I don't know what he was avoiding...

Are you saying that you think he chose to work nights to avoid having a sexual and emotional investment in you?

That's right, I don't know, but he says it's nothing to do with that. He needed to earn money. Obviously, he needed to do those things but on Saturdays, he's sleeping all day and then football. That's terrible. Dan thought Tom was leaving all the time when he was a baby. Maybe Tom just thought, "I have to work for those five years, I really want to provide," but somewhere in my head there is something else, wondering if he was punishing me. I never took his depression so seriously. He tried really to kill himself – I couldn't ever do those things…

Do you think about Christmas?

I just wonder how I'm going to cope when there is so much to do and I have so little help. How am I going to do this? I'm responsible for everything. I have to prepare everything for Dan's birthday party. I can't even say to Tom, "Go and buy…" because he doesn't know what to buy.

But his help doesn't have to be wonderful.

It doesn't have to be, no, I know. Okay, I went to buy Dan's present. And then yesterday Tom went to Hamleys and bought another one.

But that, you see, is interesting. Tom tries to help you by buying Dan's presents but you're saying, "I've already done it," so he probably feels he can't do anything right – when reactions become an automatic habit, everyone knows how hard it is for people to change.

Yes, it is difficult, especially when we started to do those things a long time ago.

So you've got three weeks before I see you again…

I want this to be a happy time for Dan.

Chapter Thirteen

January: Penny and Gillian's third response

At the third meeting with Gillian and Penny, I wondered what, if anything, there was left to say about Tom and Ingrid's determination to focus on the behaviour of their partner, instead of themselves. Except that it was frustrating. I was, of course, wrong. A great deal emerged from the discussion. While Tom and Ingrid might be taking note of the theory, how could they be persuaded to put some of it into practice?

***

Ingrid and Tom are behaving in a way that many couples do – they are each continually complaining about the behaviour of the other. In doing so they may be unconsciously projecting on to the other person how they feel about unwanted aspects of themselves. For instance, Tom says Ingrid can be cold. In turn, Ingrid says Tom won't talk about his emotions.

It might be more fruitful to reflect on the reasons for their own behaviour – to consider, for example, what parts of themselves they want to withhold and why.

For Tom, is Ingrid's alleged coldness in any way a reflection of how he holds himself back by not wishing to talk about his feelings? When Ingrid complains about Tom's desire to keep his concerns to himself – is that connected to aspects of her own emotional life, that she consciously or unconsciously keeps locked away? The climate appears to have changed between Tom and Ingrid with evidence of much more co-operation. Tom is going out less and Ingrid is making a huge effort not to raise her voice – but still there's not much evidence of reflection about their own behaviour in the way that they continue to complain in their interviews about each other.

Tom and Ingrid give the impression that each sees themselves as the victim in the relationship, with the other as persecutor and us three cast in the role of rescuers. When Tom criticises Ingrid and vice versa, it might be more constructive for him/her to first ask, "When I verbally lash out, what does that tell me about what needs of mine aren't being met?" It's as if Ingrid and Tom, at this stage in the process share a sticking-plaster approach to the marriage. They have the attitude that it can be made good enough to continue – for the sake of Dan – once the *other* person has changed his or her ways.

They each appear to believe that there's essentially one or two major causes for their problems – rooted in the past. For Ingrid, she appears to attribute a lot to Tom's upbringing and the relationship and depression he experienced as a young man. In turn, Tom suggests that Ingrid's problems might have their origins in the absence of her father when she was growing up. It's as if they are subconsciously asking us to detect the "real" cause and then Eureka! – that, once identified, the relationship will change.

We are neither rescuers nor detectives. Our role is to try and encourage Ingrid and Tom to each think about their respective behaviour in a different and hopefully more illuminating way. Then they can better analyse the chemistry (or lack of it) between themselves and make improvements. For instance, when Tom resists the temptation to stay out all night, what does he get out of that? Does he mind as much as he thought he might? Does it bring any reward – either in the way he regards himself or in the reaction from Ingrid?

When Ingrid controls her anger and avoids shouting – how does she feel when she represses her discontent? Can she find another way of expressing her view to Tom that she has to cope with too much in the home? Does she think Tom listens more when she talks or e-mails him rather than shouts?

There is a tendency for both Ingrid and Tom to give away a lot of power when they actually believe they are wielding it. Tom complains about Ingrid's shouting which makes him miserable. This gives him less power to think about his own actions. Ingrid focuses a great deal on what Tom fails to do in the house. This gives her less power to establish a boundary of behaviour for Tom that she expects him to respect.

The complexities of their relationship may also have something to do with more recent times, for instance, in becoming parents. Research shows that when a baby arrives, it requires almost constant attention. Parents can feel that they themselves have become emotionally marooned and neglected. Nobody addresses their needs, least of all the other partner who is also overwhelmed by the new offspring's demands and the new limits on freedom. So, the parents grow hurt and angry; and yet, in the presence of a helpless baby, it seems infantile and "weak" to give the reasons why – if, indeed, a parent can correctly analyse the cause of his/her unhappiness. In a relationship in which conflict has been present for several years, there is even less chance of being open and honest about feelings since this makes the partner who is forthcoming emotionally vulnerable and provides potential weaponry for the other. Instead some parents camouflage this unmet need for adult attention and they project it, instead, on to their child.

Ingrid and Tom often say they have to sort out their relationship, for Dan's sake. This may disguise the fact that, in spit of everything, they still have an attachment for each other that neither can – yet – risk acknowledging. They've got to make the relationship work because, deep down, they need each other. They can't tell each other that – so they talk about Dan. Putting Dan first sounds like a selfless act – but it may further hinder the process of reflection which can help to rebuild the relationship. This is because it places too much emphasis on changed behaviour – particularly by the other adult – and not enough on the way both Tom and Ingrid think about themselves and what they, as adults, really desire from each other.

Sex – or the lack of it – is a part of the pattern of unmet

need and projection. Ingrid seems to believe that Tom uses the withdrawal of sexual activity as a punishment. He says he isn't interested as long as she appears cold and insensitive. But both may subconsciously not wish to risk a degree of intimacy which will strip away the defences they have built up. Not least, because it may result in another area of hurt being created. Perhaps the two might consider being sensual rather than sexual? Might they engage in activity and gestures which do not necessarily have to end in sex? For instance, in cuddles, appreciation, admiration, touching, a closeness.

This, of course, requires shared, non-argumentative time together – and more focus on what they like and value about each other. In all the interviews so far, both Ingrid and Tom have given details of what they like and value in each other but to a third party. What they now need to do is tell each other.

CHAPTER FOURTEEN

Rows, change and reinvention

If one word sums up what makes a relationship weather well – it is reinvention: the ability of a couple to adapt and change, sometimes at a different pace. A friend recently decided to leave her partner after fifteen years. The reason she gave is that, once she could be honest with herself, neither he nor her had changed in the relationship since the day they first met. They'd lived a semi-detached life that she had found increasingly sterile and disconnected. For a long time, it had been a safe way for her to live, but now she wanted to risk more.

Tom and Ingrid may have initially changed a great deal – at least physically, in that Ingrid had to move countries – but emotionally they seemed to have got "stuck" very early on in the marriage. They have chosen to row rather than accommodate. Building on ideas from a paper by the US therapist Liberty Kovacs, Deirdre Morrod of One Plus One has used a developmental concept of six marital stages to help couples explore and understand how relationships change and the issues that will face them at different stages in their relationship.

The six stages are romance, reality, power struggle, finding oneself, reconciliation, and mutual respect and love. Or to put it in language we all understand – he/she's the one; god what have I done?; I hate the bastard; let's take separate holidays this year; I could do worse; and finally, I'm so lucky, I wouldn't swap him/her for the world.

The process is further complicated by external events such as the arrival of children, the mid-life crisis and changes at work. Professor John Gottman, Emeritus Professor of Psychology at the University of Washington, USA, has spent over 25 years researching couples in his Seattle "love lab" programme. Researchers videotape couples together over a period of time and observe what they say and how they behave. Professor Gottman claims to be more than 80 per cent accurate in predicting which couples will break up and which will successfully stay the course.

In an unstable marriage, Gottman says four messages are particularly negative and lead to isolation and withdrawal. He calls these, "The Four Horsemen of the Apocalypse". They are complaining/criticising, (him to her: "Why don't you support me when I make a stand with the kids?"); contempt, (her to him: "You make me sick"); defensiveness, (him to her: "That's not fair"); and stonewalling, (her to him: "I've got better things to do than argue with you all day").

In a tricky marriage, these traits will begin to emerge, almost immediately destroying respect and depleting the resources in the couple's emotional "bank". Later, when the going really gets tough, there's nothing left to draw on. Buttoning your lip isn't always easy but the way in which individuals quarrel is a habit just like any other – and all habits can be broken.

Surveys indicate that money is the issue that couples argue about the most, followed by children – not least because both tap into questions of power and control in a marriage. Couples who are more stable will hold back on some of the poison and use humour, physical overtures and reasonableness to achieve some kind of resolution. Distressed couples tend to be much more sarcastic, critical, hostile and "cold". Often, the couple will "normalise" this pattern of aggression, telling themselves it's how all couples behave. It isn't. In these highly destructive relationships, almost every fight is enacted as if it's a fight to the death. Dangerously, the verbal cut and thrust matters far more to the two individuals than the consequences of what they have said to each other. Each time, a residue of toxicity remains. This makes it difficult for peace to be brokered. As a result, rows are sparked more easily over "nothing" because each partner is disgruntled about the unsatisfactory outcome of the last spat. Eventually, life becomes just one, long, debilitating and depressing row in which the two at war recognise themselves less and less as their behaviour deteriorates. "Look, what you've done to me..." is the sad anthem of these crippled partnerships.

Women "nag" repeatedly because men fail to acknowledge how strongly they feel about a particular issue. When the men fail to respond, some wives withdraw or sulk. The men claim to be mystified. They think their wives are behaving irrationally because "it's the time of the month" – or there is some other strange, unidentified female cause. This prevents them examining their own behaviour and the real cause of the strop. Relate, the relationship organisation, suggests several ways to handle arguments constructively. Begin positively – "Can we talk about the credit card bills, please?" – not, "Don't you know anything about money?". Respect a partner's views and take responsibility for your own emotions. Ask yourself why you're so upset. If you say, "You make me so angry" it places all the blame on the other person. Be prepared to compromise. "Winning" in the short term may mean losing far more than you ever contemplated in the long run.

Many couples today – once the courtship is over – fail to find time to be together. A survey of a thousand couples published in October 2005 revealed a pattern of semi-detached relationships. One in four spent only two evenings a week in their partner's company; the bulk of their time they spent with colleagues and friends.

Some rows serve a useful purpose. They can clear the air and move the relationship to a more positive place. (He agrees to visit her mother for Christmas for the third year in a row; she agrees to have his newly divorced sister and her children for Sunday lunch every fortnight.) Some rows are rituals which paradoxically can show how well the relationship is working. (Each time they go away for a weekend, she packs enough clothes for a six-month cruise, and he argues about the unnecessary overload. Five minutes into the journey, it's all forgotten. Over time, the number of suitcases are reduced and he moans less.)

Rows are supposed to allow individuals to "get it out of their system" – some do the opposite. They fug the atmosphere and cause an overflow of bile. The arguments that can do the most damage are those that are endlessly repeated without any apparent hope of compromise or forgiveness, like Tom and Ingrid's. If the relationship involves physical and/or emotional abuse, then the best way has to be out. But otherwise, it's the precisely that ability to see a partner's point of view and to empathise – even if it is through gritted teeth – that gives the relationship the opportunity to reinvent itself.

Chapter fifteen

January: Tom's fourth interview

At the December meeting, Gillian and Penny had talked about the way in which Ingrid and Tom each gave away a lot of power when they believed they were actually wielding it. How could I encourage them both to see that pattern in action? I was also trying to resist an increasingly strong urge to abandon my alleged neutrality and give them both a good talking too.

Christmas is always a tricky scenario for the disunited and January doesn't exactly breed optimism. As I went to meet Tom, I didn't hold out much hope that, during the holiday, the couple might have turned a corner. In truth, I didn't hold much hope that the entire process was proving worthwhile.

***

TOM: Well, Christmas, blimey... Christmas was actually not. It was a bad time because I was ill and Dan was ill, then

Ingrid got a bit ill as well. I had a high temperature, Dan had chicken pox, we couldn't take him out because he was contagious, so that was not very nice. As far as I'm concerned, we were fine, from the time after Christmas to probably until a week ago. It was the best three weeks we've had for years.

Then a week ago?

It seems to build to a crescendo before she comes to meet you. It's almost as if she's anticipating the drama. I think it actually coincides with a bad time of the month as well, she does get really badly affected by that.

You think it's not a good thing then.

Well, no, it has to be done. I thought there was a real change. She wasn't shouting and we were getting on a bit better and we had a couple of chats, and then last week, it just seems to have exploded and just went right down. Last week was just awful, it was bloody awful. Both of us probably, not just me, both of us.

What triggered it.?

She's worried about me at work. I'm just not telling Ingrid about my work.

Was the row to do with jealousy?

She's gone off on one recently. I only had a few pints, but because I hadn't eaten, I came home quite pissed. I must have fallen asleep on the sofa and then in the morning, she said to me, "Where are your boxer shorts? Where are they?" I said, "What are you talking about Ingrid?" She went mad, you came home and you're on the sofa and your shorts are missing. The next day I got terrible text messages from her. I'm starting to get really stressed about it. "Ingrid, did you even look in the dirty clothes bin?" She then went quiet. She hadn't even looked in the dirty clothes basket well, I'm sure they're in there.

She didn't look in your washing basket because she said you just normally leave your clothes on the floor.

I take that on board, that's what I've been doing. We're a bloody pair we are. I can't even feel anything sometimes, I feel numb but there must be (some affection), I wouldn't be here for nothing. She's been out all night about four times, five times – did she tell you that? She's been out on the piss about four or five times with her mate all night. She's been going out a lot more than me. I just say to her, have a good night and get home safely. I say to her, make sure you stay at your friends because I'd rather she was doing that than getting a train.

Perhaps Ingrid thinks you might be having an affair?.

To me, that is an absolute joke.

Have you sat down to say that to her?

I almost think it's laughable. Do you think I'd be coming here and meeting you, while I'm having some sort of affair. It never even crossed my mind. I'm not interested in the slightest, I really don't feel attracted to other women.

Why don't you tell Ingrid not me?

I could never have an affair. What I could do is get pissed and do something stupid. I've never done that but that's the only thing I could do. I work till seven pm every day of the week and on Saturday I worked all day and [the atmosphere between us] was getting worse and worse as the week was going on, and last night I came home. Ingrid didn't answer the phone and I found out she didn't have her phone with her. So I didn't know where she and Dan were. They came home about six or seven pm, and Ingrid just went straight to bed sulking. I just thought, "I'm just going to get out of the house, I just went for a few beers."

You didn't take Dan?

I stayed with Dan, did some homework with him and stuff like that and I shouldn't have gone really, but at the same time I knew what was going to happen.

What was going to happen?

Well, we were going to have a big row. I know, I let myself concede power as Gillian and Penny suggested. I actually take that on board, I agree with that entirely. I'm giving her power. She was just pissed off for the whole week. She got more and more irate as the week went on, I don't know about what – anything, everything... There was no subject that wasn't touchy. There was nothing that wasn't going to make her angry. It was little things, big things, the contract thing. [Tom's new boss refuses to give him a contract and Tom resists Ingrid's view that he should push for one.] We had a big, screaming row about that... It's just that it isn't going to happen, so there's no point in... I just have to get on with doing my best to make sure that there's no reason for me to be sacked.

I suppose you could say Ingrid is worried about you.

I've taken so much stick over the years for everything I've done, sometimes I don't take it. She gives me shit every time I try something. I've got lots of things to do, ideas and things and I'm not so cynical. I'm quite open. I had a couple of instances where I've lost money on ventures and things I've tried, because obviously sometimes you're vulnerable. I'm in a position of weakness. He could just chuck me out tomorrow, I'm on 25 per cent of the profits and he's got a very good incentive to chuck me out. Once he gets rid of me, he's got another 25 per cent of the profits of the company.

So, going back to Sunday, Ingrid was fed up all week?

I rang home. I actually said on Saturday afternoon, after I finished work, I'll pick them up and I said let's go to the cinema, and an Italian meal afterwards, all of us, and Ingrid didn't feel like going. She wasn't dressed, didn't look right or something. She's a bit low naturally at that time of the month and she didn't want to go. So I thought, fair enough, we'll come home and eat. I couldn't get through to her on the phone. I was disillusioned with the fact that I couldn't speak to her and I hadn't seen Dan all day, I couldn't speak to him and I thought she was just playing games. I didn't know at the time she didn't have her phone with her, I thought she was just being moody.

Crossed wires – that came up last time… What happens if, instead of both of you assuming the worst of the other person's behaviour, you try assuming the best?

Yeah, it's a good spin but I just don't think it's going to happen in practice… One thing in Gillian and Penny's report, I disagree with it. I think I've mentioned to you before that, possibly it was the wrong thing to stay with Dan because of what he had to go through [with all the fighting] so I didn't see it as a selfless act. It may well be a selfish act.

They're not saying that. What they're saying is, because both

of you say, "We're doing all this for Dan," it actually gives you an excuse so you don't have to say to each other, "I want to make this work for you". Instead of resolving your own problems, you use Dan as an excuse for staying stuck.

It's a distraction. Ingrid wants another one. All through this process, and before, she says she wants another child and she's not asking me, she's telling me. "I want one, you bloody well give me one." To be honest, I don't see it's ever going to happen, I don't want it to.

Perhaps because she wants to have some physical contact with you?

I don't know. I can't argue and scream and shout all day, and then jump into bed. It's just not going to happen. We've been through that before and I can't do that.

There's another way of looking at it, that...

And it's been going on since day one, it's not something that's evolved with our relationship – she's afraid to get close

What I'm saying is that she may think that if she shows physical affection for you and you then leave her...

Yeah, but I don't know what more reassurance I can give her, I mean obviously she's afraid to get close. I've never met anyone like Ingrid. I feel pretty helpless but at the same time, I feel pretty hurt myself when it's continually happening. What have I got to do? I'm married to the girl, I haven't got to ask her for a kiss any more, sorry.

Wasn't Ingrid like that when you were going out?

Yeah, but the whole point was, I thought that would all change. I didn't like the way Ingrid was but I just thought she was being coy, I thought that was a game. I thought it was a chase thing. Once we were married, all that would go. I thought it was playful, I thought it was really funny, a really quirky character. It is quite unusual that someone would do that. I've never met anyone like Ingrid.

Is that a good thing?

It is a good thing, yes, she's unique, I see her as entirely unique and she's a one off and I love that.

So when you look at Dan...?

He's so lovely, so funny. You tell him a bus number and he says where the route starts and where it goes to. He must have 2,000 bus tickets that he's picked up. He doesn't keep them at our house, he keeps them at my mum's house...

Back to Penny and Gillian... Do you think what they've said is relevant to you or do you think they've missed the point completely?

We were in the pub the other night with Ingrid's friend and Ingrid was shit-faced when we arrived. Her eyes were rolling round her head and I thought, "My God, here we go." Ingrid told her friend about the book. Ingrid started to shout "Yvonne's going to save us," in the pub at the top of her voice...

Was that okay?...

We did have a laugh... obviously that's not true. There's no winner, in this whole thing there's no right and wrong, there's only behaviour and finding acceptance from the other person. I just thought it was a funny joke and Ingrid was laughing as well, so she can laugh about it. We *can* laugh but Ingrid is such hard work. To get a smile out of her, sometimes it's incredibly hard. I've always had no trouble making anyone have a good laugh.

So you think she's punishing you by not smiling?

Yeah, by pulling a straight, stony face sometimes. I'm smoking again, that pissed her off. She has every right to be pissed off. I'm putting the patches on. I stopped for four days and then I had a couple, and then I stopped for another few days, but I knew it was a losing battle so I just started again.

What Ingrid said to me in an email is that, he lied to me about the smoking and therefore how do I know that he hasn't had an affair?

I'm never going to do anything to Ingrid, because firstly, I know that if anything happened, that's it. We've already had so much damage in our relationship to do something like that...

This stuff about projection...

It's a nice concept. It does make sense to me. I've had a hard look at myself really. I realise that some of the things Penny and Gillian say are quite correct – I have to come that way but it's a self-defence thing.

Come what way?

Cold and... I'm probably like that myself, but I think honestly I've become like that with Ingrid because I'm just protecting myself. I'm so open, I'm easy and I'm so vulnerable. I don't know you from Adam; you could put me on the front page of the paper and destroy me tomorrow.

Why should I?

That's it – I just have to trust you because I'm throwing myself on your good nature, and I do that with people and I've done it before and I've been burned doing it, but I don't mind. I'll carry on doing it forever because that won't change those things. It's probably my best point. I've come back to this a couple of times but, if you keep trying to kiss someone and they turn away, if you keep trying to have a laugh with someone and they don't want to – if something's not right in bed, and your sex life's not right or you're not enjoying yourselves – it all adds up and, in the end...

So why do you think Ingrid wants another child?

She wants another excuse for us to stick together, which is fine but it's not the right reason to have a child, I think, because it puts Ingrid in a stronger position.

You're still talking in terms of this being a battle.

I honestly think that's my interpretation of why she wants to have a child. Why would any rational person in the middle of a marriage crisis, want to have a child? Let's be fair.

So can you have a conversation with Ingrid about this...

No, because Ingrid has made her mind up and I've made my mind up, so we just skate round this one. I'd gladly have a vasectomy tomorrow. I don't want another child from anybody and I'll never change my mind on that.

Have you told Ingrid?

The way we are, we can't have a stable relationship... one child's not enough, so you have to shout at two children?

You went out?

Yeah, that's right. I let myself down, I know that. I've been really good actually. I didn't go out, I only went out till eleven pm but, even then, I shouldn't have done it.

What about Dan?.

That's right, that's why I was really angry with myself for

doing that... I just thought Ingrid was saying to me, "Right, you've been working all day, we haven't seen you, so sod you." I was quite pissed off because I wasn't given the opportunity to do anything with them.

Supposing you'd gone about it in a different way, how would you have done it?

Well the previous Sunday, Dan and Ingrid came to the office.

She told me, she said it was really nice.

I was glad they came down. I said to them, "Come down," and Dan sat in my chair. I wanted him to come to see where daddy works. I loved it.

So you've been working all day, Ingrid's had a bad week – what might you do for her…?

I've done it before, I've made meals for Ingrid. Ingrid just says, "There's food there if you want it." I cooked Christmas dinner… Christmas Day it was just a nightmare. Ingrid's mum and her auntie and Ingrid all got pissed and they were all just screaming and shouting and crying in the kitchen, all of them.

What fighting you mean?

Her mum and her auntie. Problems came up from years ago and they were pissed and screaming and shouting and I thought, "Where have I seen this before? This looks rather familiar."

And where was Dan?

He was with me in the living room.

So he heard?

I think so. I just said to him they're just shouting and laughing and joking, but he's more intelligent than I give him credit for. I was playing with him for three or four hours. I think Ingrid's dad was a real piss-head. I think her mum said to me once, he sold the wedding ring, and drank the money or something. Ingrid keeps saying good things about her dad, he was a very handsome man. She'll shout the good things and whisper the bad things. It's obviously difficult for her.

How about you and your relationship with your father, it's interesting coming back to the issue of projecting, which is what Penny and Gillian are talking about. It never occurred to me in quite that way, but Ingrid projects on to her father and you kind of ...

She had a bitter resentment of my mum and dad, really big resentment – my mum for bringing me up the way she brought me up and my dad for not doing anything around the house and things like that. She doesn't see the fact that they never argue. They just get on so well and they're both happy in their roles. Ingrid can't accept that a woman is submissive and not unhappy and not slaving away.

Why were you unhappy with your dad when you were younger?

When you're a child I suppose, I didn't really like my dad. We didn't communicate very well, he drank too much.

Was he an alcoholic?

(Smiles) Not in the Irish sense of the word, no, they just like a drink.

Was he violent?

No, I did get the odd slap across the head but nothing ever vicious. We had some terrible rows. Once, we had a fight. I was seventeen or something. It wasn't an alcohol-dominated childhood at all – most days I should say he'd come home pissed and all that, but he wouldn't drink at home which is obviously a good thing because I never drink at home really and that's the reason I don't.

What about Ingrid?

She can't have a drink without me having a drink and I say to her, "Just enjoy a glass of wine, no problem."

It's not about that, though, it's about...

Yeah, sharing a glass of wine, but I do have a glass of wine and then I just have a glass and then she'll want to have another one and another one. She drinks wine like water, she'll drink a glass of wine as quick as someone drinks an orange juice. I'm not joking, she'll drink a glass of wine in ten minutes, no problem, and I'll be playing catch-up with her.

Can you not do something together without alcohol? You say to Ingrid, "Okay, I've got a baby-sitter, I've booked a meal and I'm not drinking alcohol because we're going to talk to each other..."

Yeah, but I think she'd look down on the whole thing.

You're being negative towards Ingrid. I think she's really taken on board that sometimes she reacts negatively. So maybe you organise an evening, if she acts negatively, write down what she says and then give it to her later... Ask her, "How am I supposed to react to something like that?"

I can see you've made a good point, I've presumed something with Ingrid and that's the problem isn't it? We're both doing it. It's just when you become familiar, and that familiarity overrides your commonsense and your normal train of thought. Now, I'm trained to think like that and that's through previous bad experiences.

But that's defensive isn't it?

Purely defensive.

It's as if both of you are waiting for the other person to land the first punch which means you're defensive and negative with each other all the time.

That's right, yes, defences down in other words. I did it the other week. I went out and I actually thought "I can't go home because I'll just get some stupid remark" and that stopped me going back home.

What if you'd gone back and said, "I've come back because I want this relationship to work and I love you and I love Dan and what we're doing is destroying ourselves." If you did that, what's the worst thing Ingrid could say?

The other issue is that sometimes, I don't know what I feel any more, I don't know if I love her. Obviously, I must do somewhere.

You don't have sex, you argue all the time, you hardly see each other, it's amazing that you're even involved in this [year-long project].

(Smiles) It is incredible isn't it? I've taken some things on board that you've said tonight. Definitely, I'm prepared to confront all my demons, everything. I'm prepared to read all sorts of crap and take it on board, I am. But it's how much I really want to do, isn't it? And how much do I think I should do it? Because there's a big difference between knowing the right things to do and the motive for doing them.

Why did you engage in this then?

I don't know what's going to develop out of it. I'm not going to wait for a magic cure. What I'm waiting for is to understand my real feelings towards Ingrid, because there's so much gone on. I feel totally numb about Ingrid sometimes, just totally numb, I don't know what to think.

You feel numb about somebody that you've chosen. Does that say something about her or something about you?

No, perhaps me as well, it's a very difficult one to interpret, just using the word projection.

Do you pre-empt her leaving you by you leaving her? Ingrid has stopped shouting hasn't she?

Yes, last week, she's been brilliant. I was really pleased and proud, I still think it's good, I'm not going to give up just because of this week. I've not been sleeping properly the last couple of weeks, I've been absolutely physically and mentally drained and shattered .

Why?

Well, pressure of work. I've literally got twenty things to do at once at work

Why don't you involve Ingrid?

Well, I always tell her what I'm doing at work but I just think…

Ingrid texts you a lot doesn't she?

Yes, quite offensively often. "You effing B" was the last one I think.

Is she trying to hold contact with you?

Well, she rings up. I find it really funny because we can have just had a blazing row and she'll go, "How are you?" She hides behind the phone and hides behind an email and we can have a great conversation when we can't see or hear each other.

What Penny and Gillian are saying is that you both are reacting always to what the other person is doing and saying, You're not actually addressing your own behaviour much... It's like a war of attrition.

Honestly, I wake up in the morning and it's rush, rush, rush. I've got to get things ready for work. It has been incredibly stressful. I've been going to bed early, I want to get into a routine, I want to get on top of things properly, so it's going to take a little while.

Do you say any of this to Ingrid?

Well, I don't think I have actually, no. I think I should have done but at the same time, I don't know. I've said to her before, to get her and Dan into a routine. I'm rushing back from work at 7.30 picking Dan up. So I get home at 8.00... it's 12 hours since I left the house and then Dan's got to do his homework and then he has to have some time to play with me. The benefit of my new job is going to be that I'll say to Ingrid, "You don't have to go to work any more."

It's interesting that you say you're conflicted about how you feel about her at the same time as you're planning a future with her.

I'm just bloody mad aren't I? I am planning, yes. It's not in my nature to give up.

You gave up on the woman who was in your early life.

No, I don't think that was a case of giving up, I would just say it was a sensible thing to do.

151

You disguise your commitment to Ingrid and Dan in other words.

Yeah, it's not an issue for me to think about divorcing Ingrid, until I've exhausted everything. I'm planning the future still, yes. I have told Ingrid everything I feel, about how our marriage is crap, but I said to her, I really want to make a go of this. We've made love a couple of times and a couple of things happened and we had a good chat. So I could see potential but at the same time, it's going to take a lot. It's weird isn't it – how we could appear to be trying so hard and at the same time be doing so little.

Gillian and Penny suggested that you could try being sensual rather than sexual.

It's harder to be sensual than sexual isn't it? It's harder. Sexual is easy in some respects, men have their brains in their underpants don't they? So it's easy to be sexual, isn't it? The hard part is being sensual for a bloke, isn't it? I think they are asking more than they realise.

It applies to Ingrid as much as it does to you.

Ingrid doesn't do sensual.

You could talk to each other about it.

Yeah, I think I have to be more open and candid about these issues really. I don't talk because I've been hurt by them and so I suppose I avoid them. Blokes don't talk.I used to put my arm around Ingrid and muck about and kiss her and hug her. I used to do all those things, but gradually, things evolved, so your reactions change. I can't keep giving and giving and giving, you just get so emotionally slaughtered, it's a really terrible thing. You're getting nothing back, eventually the well goes dry. I think it's incredible that we're still together. Christ, if you knew what we were like, if you knew that w'd had sex probably ten times in two years, you just wouldn't believe it. The whole thing about mucking around and having fun and playing around, just silly things… You only do them when you're happy.

Why don't you ask Ingrid about that? Why don't you have a conversation with her?

Well, we don't talk about things. I look back on my behaviour. I took redundancy and think I've been very, very selfish. I used to work all the time and I used to go out for a beer and I used to think, "Well, I deserve a bloody beer." But I became indulgent since I left work and Ingrid's behaviour was my excuse for my own indulgence. I'm going to put that right now. There are going to be big changes. I've already started, I haven't been out till after one am in the morning since Christmas, Boxing Day.

It's interesting: what you've sort of said is, unless you have work, you don't trust yourself to behave… For instance, you chose to work nights.

You say I chose to work nights, I didn't have a choice in that. I know Gillian and Penny will look at it in a different way but I honestly feel that that was not a choice. I had to earn.

Why wasn't the connection with the baby stronger?

In what regard?

Because you were sleeping when he was awake.

You know, I worked bloody ridiculous hours, and all I got for it was abuse.

That's what I'm saying. You have a really strong relationship

153

with Dan now and yet, then, you were prepared to sacrifice your time with him?

Well, I wasn't prepared to do it, I had to do it, I accepted that's what was going to happen because otherwise we weren't going to be in our flat anymore and that was just not going to happen.

Do you think honestly that is …

It's obscene.

I don't know about obscene but it's also a very good camouflage for not facing up to life.

Yes, it is but... if she was earning more money. I didn't want to do those hours.

There's loads and loads of people who earn a decent living who don't have to do that.

Not in London, not when your partner's not working. I'm not accepting that Yvonne, I'm really not.

This is what Gillian and Penny might say, that you really have to examine, deep down, what that was really about. You had a young baby, clearly you're a really good father, you have a good relationship with Dan and you opted out for several years?

Well, I don't think that's fair on me, I really don't… I mean, obviously we weren't happy in our relationship. We could have had a council place – I don't want that, blimey, but the fact is, it would have been cheaper… and I wouldn't have had to work that hard.

What stopped that?

Well, Ingrid didn't want to go in a council flat. It's stigmatised. At the same time, "Sod that Ingrid, let's look at reality."

Okay, so that's interesting: Ingrid took the decision?

That's right, that's why I don't accept it, Yvonne, I've been over this so many times. She said, "I'm not going to work for three months," so I said, "That's fine, I understand that but I'm going to have to work harder if you don't work." So she made the choice. You have to see from my side as well.

I do see it.

But Ingrid sees it as though I decided to go and work these ridiculous long hours because I love working 18 hours a day... I used to stay up, even when I got home and I was shit tired. I'm quite creative, so I wrote a letter to a big advertising firm, and I got an interview with their top man. I wrote quite a funny poem actually... Basically I thought of some ideas for a drink-drive ad campaign. He said, "That's quite good." I said, "No, it's not quite good, it's very good" – and he wouldn't have it. He said, "You can't just come in here and get a job." I said, "Why can't I?" I said, "Give me something you're working on now to advertise and I'll go away and work it up" and he said, "No." I said, "Well give me some stuff that you've worked on before, that you want me to advertise and I'll come up with something better." He said "No." There was a big can of Pepsi in the corner because they did the campaign for Pepsi... I said, "If you want me to come up with something better than that..."– he didn't really like that.

But it didn't work for you did it?

No, it didn't work for me.

You didn't get what you wanted.

No, I didn't get what I wanted.

Winning points in the short-term is not the same as achieving what you might want in the long-term.

But the whole point is that I've never given up trying to do other things. I've got inventions in my head that I haven't acted on for years. I'm certain I'll get one done eventually when I've got time.

Is it better financially now for the two of you?.

It's going to be difficult for a while, but we're fine. If I'm not earning six figures by the end of next year, something's severely wrong – I'm in a fair amount of debt... I've got quite a bit of debts I must admit on credit cards, but I'll deal with that... It's £20,000, something like that.

That adds to the pressure doesn't it?

Of course, I have to do well. That's why I'm working seven days a week. If do fuck up, it won't be for want of trying.

CHAPTER SIXTEEN

February: Ingrid's fourth meeting

O ne of the issues that Penny and Gillian and I had discussed but not yet passed on to Tom and Ingrid is their
difference in age. Ingrid is five years older and this, perhaps,
has also made her more reflective than Tom. On several
occasions, she had referred to a mid-life crisis. Tom had said
Ingrid had asked if he was having an affair – might this be
Ingrid projecting on to Tom a secret wish of her own? My
instinct is that neither is being unfaithful. On the other hand,
since they live such separate lives, anything is possible.

***

It's easier for me. Tom is working and he's happier. He went
out and Dan was in our bed. Tom came in, he went to sleep
on the sofa. I thought that was strange, I could tell by his
body language. I said to him, "Why didn't you come to bed?
Are you doing something? Why react like this?" He was

defensive. I told him, "I'm going to find out one day anyway." I went to pick up his underwear. Normally, he just drops it on the floor and it wasn't there. I said, "Where's your underwear?" He got really cross. He said, "Do you think I've left them with a prostitute or something?" He said, "I don't want any stress."

You said before that you didn't think he would have an affair.
I don't know 100 per cent. I think he's faithful; ten per cent I wonder. Do you know he's started smoking again. I can't believe it! My mum came to our house and I saw the mouth freshener in the cupboard so I knew. My mum asked him and he said, "I've never smoked" and I knew he'd already started! I said, "How can you lie like that... so easily? I'm ashamed of you." Tom said "Don't be angry, be supportive, this is a stressful time..." If he can lie about this, he can lie about anything, that's what I think. He's had so many opportunities [to have an affair]. He's a young man. Things don't add up.

Are you a jealous person?
Not jealous, jealous... but his brother had an affair.

Picking up on what Penny and Gillian said in their last report, are you perhaps projecting something about yourself on Tom? Would you want to have an affair?
Maybe....I don't know *(shrugs)*. After the first report [when there was a reference to having an affair] we talked a bit about what was written and Tom said he would understand if I had, but I wouldn't like him to, no way...

How long have you been thinking this way... about whether he might be having an affair?

About three weeks ago... Things are better between us but still, he's working a lot so we don't have that much time together. He doesn't go out and drink so much because he can't afford to wake up with a hangover when he has to go to work. You know, if I came home late, I'd go to my bed not the sofa. It's cold and uncomfortable. There's something...

Are your instincts usually good?

My instincts are usually good. He says I'm complex but he's the difficult one, not me. Perhaps it's me? Is it me? Sometimes, I wonder if I'm going mad. Sometimes, I think he can convince me of anything...

Have you always worried about him having an affair – you haven't talked about that before?

I've always had a five per cent when I thought – sometimes, I ask him, "What have you been doing?" Sometimes, I think "I don't know you..." Tom says that I'm cold but he hasn't been there for me ever.

Did your mother say anything about the two of you at Christmas?

It was easier. We had friends around. Tom said I was different. He doesn't go out so much and when he does go out we don't argue so much. This morning he was cross. He said "Where's the fucking..." – Tom uses more bad language than me.

Where was Dan?

He was in the living room. I don't know if he heard. I went and told him it was all right.

Do you still feel angry?

Well, we do talk more. We do talk. When I've asked him

about the affair, he said [if that was happening] why would I be doing this [the book] with you? He asks me why I keep talking about the past. I do want to talk about the future but first I need to sort out the first five years. Otherwise, it's like a block. We are beginning to discuss it all a little bit more. Perhaps this is a new chapter.

Do you talk to your sister about Tom?

Not since December. She and her husband have been to a summer camp for married people. They have been twice. They share all their problems with everybody. I'm not that kind of person. She's given me lots of books which I read. I've given them in English to Tom. I wish he would read them. Two years ago, she gave me books on counselling but Tom's not interested. If Tom did have an affair that would be it. I'd say to myself, this man is not for me, I'd leave because it would be happier for Dan – but I'm not giving up yet. If I did find out about an affair it would be very difficult. I could forgive but not forget.

In the evenings, do you have time together now?

Tom comes home at about 7.30pm. I cook, or he cooks. Twice a week he picks up Dan from his mother – but it's all getting too late for Dan.

Does Dan miss his dad now he's working?

He doesn't say much. I tell him it isn't going to last forever, it's daddy's new job... Sometimes, there is still tension between us. Before, Tom used to stay up until one am and I would go to bed early because I was knackered. Now he's going to bed early, too. We are talking better to each other...

Are you showing affection to each other more?

I think I'm more demonstrative. I have to ask him for a cuddle. At home when he's happy, he gives me a cuddle. But sometimes, if I ask he gets stressed.

Do you think you misread each other?

Yes, definitely. I came home the other evening and there was Dan's porridge still on the kitchen table. I was so angry. It takes one minute to put the dish in the sink so why can't Tom do it? He says he's easy-going and I'm the difficult one but I think he's the complex one. I think the biggest problem is how he was brought up. I know my background is something to do with my mother. You ate something and then you put the dish away. His mother will do it all. I don't want to nag about these stupid things. But they do matter. It's about showing that you care; it's about men and women sharing...

Is that what some of this is about – trying to work out how to be a couple, making up your own rules about who does what?

Well, I pay for everything for Dan. It's not about money when Tom has it, he is always generous. When I'm out with a [girl]friend, he says "Stay overnight..." I do that about once a month. I went with a girlfriend to the theatre and to drinks. It was midnight when we came out. I phoned Tom and he was really angry. He wanted to know where I was and who I was with. When I told him, he told me to go and stay with her. She has a place in the King's Road. I was working the next day. We are quite similarly jealous if we have reason to be. Sometimes, I wonder if I'm having a mid-life crisis? I'd like to have one more child but in this situation I think no, then I think yes. Tom says it's not fair to bring a child into the world because the world is so bad... Everyone asks about another baby. Two weeks ago, I wanted one; now I don't know...

Would you perhaps go away together now?

I suggested that we go away together to Italy for my birthday. Tom immediately said, "Let's take Dan". So Dan came... It was nice but it wasn't the same. I call Tom three times a day, to ask "How's it going?" He says, "I'm so busy, I can't talk now.." He always says, "I'm so busy....." So I text him, sometimes a lot.

How is your work going?

I've been there four years in April. I always leave after four years. I'm bored. So bored. I want to do something else but the hours are good. It's a good job.

Do you feel you're on a bit of a treadmill?

Sometimes. Last weekend, Anna [a friend] and I were in the pub and drunk a bottle of champagne each when Tom and her boyfriend came. We were a little bit drunk but we were laughing so much. [Anna is a Scandinavian friend who has returned home. This was a farewell evening.] We went to our place and we all had fun together. [Ingrid then returns to her concerns about Tom possibly having an affair]. I put two things together. I can see his body language.

Perhaps sometimes, we see what we want to see?

Perhaps I want to see him having an affair? I don't know if I'd leave. It's not the affair. I'm more worried about truthfulness. I'd stay because I've no money to go anywhere. But if I did stay, I'd never have sex and I'd stay for a short time only. I would go to his mum and tell them. I've always told Tom that I would tell them. But how would I tell my boss and people who know us who think we are fine? Me and Dan would move to my country. But it's difficult for me to say we'd go. Dan loves his father.

Isn't that what Penny and Gillian are suggesting? You think you are wielding power – but if Tom has been unfaithful to you and you stay, you're going to stay without sex or money – that's punishing you, isn't it, not him?

(Nodding) I've read lots of books to do with my past. I can see what I'm doing wrongly. I say to Tom, how can I give you anything, if you're not going to give me something in return? *(Near to tears)* I know how he feels. He's more sensitive than he tells me... He talks about me being cold. The night before I came to live in England, I didn't sleep. I was full of questions...What have I done? What am I leaving behind? On the plane, a man began to talk to me. He was walking with me through the gates and I was worried what Tom would think – and he did ask about who the man was and how we met. I was cold because I was worried and I had things on my mind.

Tom wanted you to behave in a certain way? Perhaps more like his mother might behave?

I don't know, sometimes he doesn't like his mum. He likes his sister and she is very different. When I met Tom I thought he was a new age man. He did change Dan's nappies at first and got up but when we had a baby he couldn't see what I needed. It's true what Gillian and Penny say, I needed my space, too, but I couldn't because Tom decided to work nights. He had a choice and he didn't choose us. I began to think who is this man? Sometimes, I don't know.

Gillian and Penny were suggesting that perhaps as couples we

underestimate the lack of attention we each receive once a baby arrives and we become parents?

I think that's right. I'm not only a parent. I tell Tom we should be together more but what can I do? We have no time and no money. On Valentine's, Tom can't think ahead and surprise me. He doesn't book a restaurant table. I always think of those things. Sometimes, I come in and before I even sit down, he says, "Okay, can you put Dan to bed..." I say, "Let's wait..." Dan goes to bed at 8.30, 9 o'clock... I don't know what I'm doing wrong when I come in... He's been telling me all these years that I'm difficult but he's talking about himself. Thursday, we had an argument. We had guests coming on Saturday. Why can't he say, "Can I help you? Is there anything I can do?" I joke that Tom has the same birthday as Hitler; he uses me as a slave. He should say, "Can I help?" I was washing dishes late and he was watching TV. It's just the little things. If he said, "Can I do anything?", I'd say no but it's asking. He doesn't think like that and it makes me so mad.

CHAPTER SEVENTEEN

February: Gillian and Penny fourth response

O ver the first few meetings with Ingrid and Tom, guided by Gillian and Penny, I had begun to understand how the couple's lives as children were influencing their relationship now. Ingrid seems to have a very idealised image of marriage since she was reared in a lone parent family. Hence, perhaps, her quest for "perfection".

Tom, in turn, had repeatedly hinted at money worries and difficulties at work – yet he had confided very little of this to Ingrid. Tom's father had been depicted as a traditional bread-winner. As the head of the house he too, presumably, would have kept financial problems and work issues – if he'd had any – to himself. But Tom's unwillingness to share seemed to underline for Ingrid that they were not working together "perfectly" as a team; she was marginal to his life. It was not such a big step for her to then believe that some other woman was in this special position, sharing confidences and her bed with Tom. In different ways, there was an element of the unreal about both Ingrid and Tom's expectations of their marriage. Could Gillian and Penny explain why? And how could the couple be persuaded to come back down to earth and develop a relationship that was good enough for the here and now, not some time in the future when Tom's business plans might achieve success?

***

The therapeutic process works in three stages – exploring, understanding and, finally, resolving. While there appear to have been positive changes in Ingrid and Tom's relationship – the exploring has come to an end but the understanding and the compromises that have yet to begin. Instead, there is some repetition of describing the other's faults, almost as if both Ingrid and Tom are stalling– delaying the time when they have to change their own behaviour for the long term. One of the penalties involved in beginning to understand why and how the relationship is working – or failing to work – is a sense of disappointment. The person they know now is recognised as very different from the idealised person they married. The key question is, can each person adjust and compromise to this reality? Can they see any value in what the other person offers now – and the rewards that may come in future from adaptation and a life shared?

Some people believe that that degree of disappointment is catastrophic. The person they "see" now is not the person they wish to spend years with in future. However, before making that decision, it's sometimes useful to ask a few questions. Is the person you think you want impossible to find? Second, how much is the other person the cause of your own unhappiness and discontent? Is some of your unhappiness and discontent to do with yourself? A sign of maturity is the ability to recognise that no relationship is perfect. It is possible for two people to rediscover each other in a more realistic, resilient and mutually supportive way. In a study of happiness published in 2005, Professor Andrew Clark suggested that, "Happiness is not getting what you want, it's wanting what you have."

The "good enough" relationship often means accepting that the ordinary, the routine, "the beauty of everydayness" to quote one study on relationships, also offers many pleasures. Both Ingrid and Tom perhaps want themselves and the other person to be "very special". But specialness is a precarious state. If you find your self on a pedestal, often the only way is down. What if Ingrid and Tom each discovered that the other is ordinary – as are most of us? Neither of them appear to live in the present very much, appreciating what they have now. Instead, they both seem to believe that much will be improved between them in the future when Tom begins to make money; when Ingrid works less; if there is a second child, a new house. It might be useful to look at their relationship in the context of the worst scenario becoming fact: what if Tom's business venture fails? Would he be good enough for Ingrid as he is?

On one level, Ingrid and Tom's behaviour appears quite reckless, perhaps that's a reflection of their unhappiness. They have debts. By the standards of many couples, they live well

– eating out, drinks, taxis, clothes. Could they cut back; lower their sights; enjoy more of what is simple, ordinary and inexpensive together; inject more calm into their lives?

Tom insists that long hours are essential for his family's prosperity but that time doesn't have to deflect from his (or Ingrid's) contribution to creating a calm routine on a daily basis. There isn't much relaxation in the home – it's as if Ingrid and Tom are always preparing for the next party – but when the party happens, they don't know how to enjoy it as a couple, unless alcohol is involved. Of course, drink relaxes but it also fuels aggravation and, instead of bringing them together, it seems to widen the distance between them at times. Both are afraid: of failure, of loss, and of losing control. Alcohol helps to drown the fear.

Perhaps as part of the process of understanding themselves it would be useful if they each examined who they are and of what they are most afraid? What would their worst enemy say about them? What would their biggest admirer say about them? Once they can risk being honest about themselves, they may look at their partner's "faults" and realise that some of them are also what they least like about themselves. It's at that point that Tom and Ingrid might hear the click! that opens the door to greater understanding.

***

Observations not shown to Tom and Ingrid at the time –
Ingrid may be more able to "see" Tom and accept him for who he is – although she is seeking a powerful archetypal

father/husband/protector. Perhaps she needs to accept her own strengths a bit more. Tom has a strong inferiority complex – he's frightened of being clobbered, always waiting for the next blow to fall. He may have an unrealistic view of debts/prospects. Both are perhaps unduly concerned about what others think – that may hinder their capacity to look honestly at themselves. Both are concerned that the behaviour of the other person is out of control when they are really troubled about their own behaviour – eg Tom's smoking, Ingrid's drinking. Tom is ambivalent. He encourages Ingrid to go out and drink but then is not happy when she passes out. Perhaps, unconsciously, this is because his own sobriety indicates to him that he is "better" than her.

It's ironic that Ingrid complains about Tom not picking up after himself – yet when he comes home drunk and does put his boxer shorts in the laundry basket she accuses him of infidelity. The issue of sex also seems to be a case of role reversal. Ingrid is asking for more sex (usually the male role) while Tom is seeking more affection and warmth (usually the female role). Tom wants a princess; Ingrid wants a prince. His choice of a woman from a different culture also makes Ingrid appear special.

Chapter Eighteen

Parents, and what they do to our love lives

Doreen Davis is 56, married for 32 years, a mother and grandmother and ex-teacher. Her husband, David is a former candidate for the leadership of the Conservative party and she is also his constituency secretary. For the past three decades, she has devoted herself to creating a home for her husband and children.

"I suppose I come last in the priority of things", she said cheerfully, when describing her marriage.

She lives in Yorkshire, while her husband spends a great deal of time in London. "David is the basis of everything. I work for him as well as being married to him. Everything is bound up in him really... Often days go by and we don't speak on the phone. Life becomes a bit separate because you get used to doing your own thing. There was passion to start with in our marriage but I suppose that goes after 32 years..." The couple met at university. "I felt secure with him. I felt that he would look after me. I suppose he was always in charge. I just assumed our marriage would be something similar to my parents."

Research tells us that we internalise the experience of the first couple in a relationship we know – our parents. "Marion", happily married for over 30 years, explains how her choice of partner was moulded by similar influences to those that directed her mother: "She was married three times and eventually settled for my dad, an emotional paraplegic but as solid as a rock. She told me that, when you change partners, you take your problems with you, not leave them behind. Her spirit was depleted by always moving on."

In her twenties, Marion had two proposals from Rob and Mark. Rob reminded her of a Joni Mitchell song "Hot, hot blazes come down to smoke and ashes..."

"Mark was loyal and kind and he adored me. I wanted to have children and I knew that if I had, say, a blind baby, Mark would be the one at home, by my side, while Rob would be straight into his leather trousers and off to the wine bar. At the time I felt I was settling for Mark but after all these years, I know how bloody lucky I've been. Mark is my best friend. Of course, he can be incredibly tedious and irritating but he is also amusing, honest, solid. We share a history. You can have a bad day together or month or even a year but it's how you frame the problems that count. It's like the drop of ink in the glass of water. The whole glass goes blue. You can chuck it out and say, it's not good. Or you can say, it's only a drop of ink, we'll survive. Being positive helps."

Tom and Ingrid have grown up in two very different types of household. Ingrid was reared by an independent self

-supporting woman. Tom has grown up with a traditional model of marriage. Several times in interviews, he has said that relationships have a greater chance of working well if one partner is "submissive" – nor does he believe that is a role automatically filled by the woman. For instance, he describes his brother-in-law as submissive.

Professor John Gottman has identified three types of marriage: validating, volatile and avoidant. Validators, according to Gottman, are often found in "old fashioned" marriages in which one or other partner is more "submissive", a description that appears to apply to Tom's parents as well as Doreen and David Davis. If validators don't agree on an issue, they try to argue their case with good humour; they each air their grievances then eventually reach a compromise.

Often these couples have stereotypical sex roles – the wife is in charge of home and children; the husband sees himself as the "final decision-maker". Validators value the "we-ness" of their marriage over individual goals and values. They may finish each other's sentences. They consider "what's mine is yours" and place interests in common above a life apart. While the family is often the focus of the women's lives, the men have a life outside domesticity. Gottman warns that validating couples may turn their marriage into a "passionless arrangement in which romance and selfhood are sacrificed for friendship and togetherness... forgoing personal development in favour of keeping their bond strong."

In Gottman's description of Volatile Couples, the roles are much more fluid. These couples argue to win, not to hear the other person's point of view but they will, eventually, reach a compromise. They may be more turbulent but they are also more passionate and fun-loving than validating couples. Volatile couples see themselves as equals. They believe marriage should reinforce their individuality. At home, they have separate spaces and respect each other's privacy. They constantly contradict and interrupt each other. They are open about their emotions and censor few of their thoughts, a facility which can also take a couple to a dangerous zone. These relationships can be as solid as those of validating couples, Gottman says, so long as they, "keep steady amidst the high winds of passion".

Avoidant couples, as the label implies, avoid conflict. They don't air grievances, "they agree to disagree". They accentuate the positive in their relationship, and accept the rest as part of the package. They lead calm, pleasant lives and value their separateness. The danger is that when real conflict does arrive, they aren't equipped to handle it in a way each regards as "safe". Issues become buried. Avoidant couples take the risk of loneliness within the relationship. One may feel the other doesn't really know or understand him or her.

All three types, according to Professor Gottman, can create long-lasting relationships (and some couples, of course, may weave all three types of behaviour into their partnership). How they do it, and what makes the difference between reasonably contented couples and those who aren't, is what he calls "the magic ratio" of positivity to negativity. Five to one works. As long as there is five times more positive feelings and interactions between the two individuals than there are negative, then no matter how loud, noisy, acquiescent or "submissive" – the relationship will be viewed as successful by both parties. All relationships need some negativity, anger and differences. These encourage a cycle of closeness and distance that can renew love and affection and stimulate desire. In reconciling, courtships aren't just rekindled but often move on to a deeper level.

How people behave towards each other is habitual. In a busy, pressured life it's easy to fall out of the habit of signalling to the other person that he or she really matters. Gottman offers a list of ways to encourage more positivity: be polite; show interest; be affectionate; be appreciative; show concern; be accepting (you respect your partner's view even if you don't agree with it); enjoy a joke and express your pleasure or happiness. These simple rules of behaviour need to be an integral part of a relationship from the outset to give it half a chance of flourishing.

Some couples do observe the positive " rules" instinctively – perhaps because, as children, they were programmed by witnessing a similar kind of relationship between their parents. Others have to acquire the technique. This is further complicated if it's only one half of the partnership that's doing the trying. The romance and etiquette of a marriage may be eroded over the years simply because we forget to fan the flames that sparked the relationship in the first place. Love left to get on with it rarely looks after itself well.

CHAPTER NINETEEN

March: Tom and Ingrid joint fifth meeting

Tom and Ingrid decided they wanted to be interviewed together because Ingrid had become increasingly unhappy about what Tom might be saying about her. The issue of confidentiality had also arisen. Tom was concerned that Ingrid was talking to her family about the interviews and the book. Gillian and Penny and I also believed that it was in Dan's best interest that his parents shouldn't be identified. I met Tom and Ingrid at their flat. Dan was at his grandparents. Given that the two were still sticking to their own list of grievances about the other, I couldn't see how this meeting would change the situation. I was wrong. The interview moved us all into a different and potentially frightening place – but would it also provide a real chance of improvement in the relationship?

***

INGRID: I want to be more open. okay, I shouldn't have read that first e-mail but it wasn't the truth. If someone reads the book and it's not true that worries me. We need to communicate more. Last Thursday, St Patrick's Day, he didn't want to stay with me – and I didn't ask.

You're worried about what Tom has said about you?

INGRID: Yes, not because of the book but because I want to know what he thinks: why he hates me. That first e-mail was just rubbish – it wasn't true. I have to prove to myself that I'm not that person.

What I think Gillian and Penny are saying is that actually what people say isn't only what they are interested in. It's also why you are saying it. What does it signal beyond the surface meaning?

INGRID: What he said about my mum. He doesn't even know my mother, she can't even speak English, so how can they communicate? He says to me, "Oh, there must be something wrong with you..."

You're not going to correct the other person's behaviour until you look at how you behave yourselves. Most people involved in a relationship who are trying to stay together as you are, are looking for solutions. Gillian and Penny are trying to say that it's about adjusting to reality. The person you met and fell in love with is not the person you're with now. And you have to decide whether you want to be with that person. It's very difficult to make that decision when there's so much hostility.

INGRID: He doesn't want to stay here. He doesn't want to talk. He says such stupid things.

TOM: They're not stupid.

INGRID: *(distressed)* The normal thing is to talk, otherwise I will end up killing you.

You're saying you need to be able to express yourself more?

INGRID: Yes, when I came here I wanted to be open – put all our cards on the table, lots of talking...

TOM: *(interrupts)* Can I just say something? Firstly, I haven't been going out nearly as much as I used too.

INGRID: Yes, that's true, you haven't.

TOM: Can we establish that I've changed my behaviour?

INGRID: You went out three times last week.

TOM: If you remember, I went to a meeting.

INGRID: *(interrupts)* Then you went out after work on Thursday.

To be honest who stays in and who stays out is the least of your problems – the question is...

TOM TO INGRID: *(angrily)* But once is too much for you, isn't it, Ingrid? – if I go out at all? It's always negative when I go out. When you go out I say, "Have a nice time"; when I go out I get...

INGRID: Honestly, go, go – but you're always abandoning me and Dan. He's always saying, "Where's daddy?"

TOM: It's not quite like that, Ingrid. When you're out I don't say you're abandoning Dan.

INGRID: We went to his brother's home – normally Tom doesn't drink because we go by car but obviously I can have a couple of drinks then.

TOM: *(interrupts)* A couple?

INGRID: Okay, your family pour all the glasses of wine. Okay, I drank. But anyway every time we come home he goes out afterwards. You never want to stay with me.

TOM: When was the last time I did that? When was the last time I did that?

INGRID: Every time – for seven years all the time.

TOM *(growing angry)* When was the last time, Ingrid? When was the last time? It was months ago.

Hold on, you're both forever going back to what happened years ago.

INGRID: Every time we've been out, Tom says – *(exasperated)* "Oh my God! I'm going to go out now, bye bye!". He takes his car and goes somewhere. He wants to go out with his mates. Every time.

TOM: Can I say something? That night we got in the car – it was quite a nice evening but, all through the evening, Ingrid was sniping and making comments. Just little things designed to make my brother and his wife...

INGRID: What are you talking about? What did I say?

TOM: Okay, so we got in the car and got to the house. You were quite drunk in my opinion.

INGRID: *(interrupts)* We were eating and we had wine.

TOM: I let you speak; will you be quiet when I speak? You said Dan shouldn't sit in the front seat of the car and that's the moment you just went mad. You were screaming and screaming in front of Dan for about an hour.

INGRID: *(Inaudible)* Don't be so stupid.

TOM: Ingrid, Dan was crying and crying and he heard every word you said.

INGRID: No, he was sleeping.

TOM: I barricaded the door with a chair to stop you

smashing the door down.

INGRID: Dan was in bed, Dan was sleeping.

(Ingrid and Tom talk over each other with increasing volume)

INGRID: It's not true. It's not true.

Hold on, when people are in conflict there's not usually a truth they can agree on. You each have a different view of the truth so, no matter how much you keep correcting each other, that isn't going to change.

TOM: It doesn't work like that.

INGRID: He has to be at home, that's the whole problem.

Okay so we still have the recurring problem of Dan hearing you argue?

TOM: I was so angry with Ingrid for exploding at Dan in the car. It made him cry right away. He was crying. I said, "Get in the back Dan cos mummy's upset."

INGRID: Oh my God!

Whoa, say nothing just give each other a chance.

TOM: We got here and I tried to be quiet, not to continue it and I said to Ingrid "There's no point in talking to you now, you're drunk – you're screaming at me, we can't have a conversation." Whether it's Ingrid or me or both of us, Dan shouldn't be hearing it. So I shut this [sitting-room] door and put the chair in front of it. Ingrid is trying to smash the door in.

INGRID: Oh, I did not!

TOM: Ok forcing the door. Ingrid came into the bedroom and said horrible things about my dad. I couldn't believe what I was hearing and that was the end for me. I didn't want to speak to her. I turned my mobile off [the next day]. The next night my dad brought Dan to meet me at the station and I felt bad.It's something more than something said in a fit of temper. I still can't accept it. I need some sort of complete retraction. I'm really not happy. I can't go on. I just think it's way beyond anything I've ever heard in my life.

INGRID: What about what you say about my family? You are always saying something must have happened in my past because you say I wake up screaming.

TOM: No, I'm just worried honestly because you never stop screaming.

INGRID: Do you know what it was like for me when I came to this country? When I came to your parents? I couldn't trust anybody here, could I?

TOM: Why not? Why not?

Isn't this really about hurting each other as much as you can? I mean, when you're pissed, you say things they don't mean.

TOM: It went way beyond that for me.

INGRID: I can't say anything about your parents but you can say anything about my parents

TOM: But I don't.

INGRID: Yeah, yeah. You tell me things. I've never said anything about your dad because I don't know your dad.

TOM: I don't know what you're talking about.

INGRID: I'm fucking angry that's why. I'm so angry with you.

TOM: Ever since I first met you, you've done that [shouting in her sleep].

INGRID: It's a joke in my family. I've always been like that always. It's nothing to do with us Tom, it's nothing to do with us.

TOM: But you've been doing it for seven years. You don't know how bad it is because you're dreaming when you do it. I'm the one who sees how terrifying it seems for you

INGRID: That's not true because you never say, "Oh God, what can I do? How can I help?" You're really angry every time.

TOM: You don't know how bad it is in the middle of the night when you're screaming. In the dead of night when you wake up and someone is screaming full volume, it's really scary.

INGRID: It's not that bad…

(Ingrid and Tom both raise their voices and shout at each other)

Do you know what's happening – neither of you is listening to the other at all?

TOM: I'm concerned.

INGRID: You don't have to be concerned.

TOM TO YVONNE: This is how we normally are.

I don't know why you bother because you're not getting any-where. You're not listening to each other.

INGRID: I know, this has gone on for so many years. We sit in front of the television, not speaking.

It's not that you haven't spoken. You are speaking to each other without saying anything, both of you – because you're so defensive.

INGRID: Yes we are, we are.

Tom isn't actually saying to you that you're waking up at night because of the state of the marriage, he's saying you were doing it right from the beginning

INGRID: Yes that's right.

But you're saying he's saying it's caused by the marriage – and

181

Tom's not listening to you either.

TOM: I'm agreeing with you. I'm worried about you because...

INGRID: Worried about me? No way.

TOM: I'm worried. I'm just worried about why it's happening.

INGRID: It's because I'm angry with you.

TOM: If that was the truth it would be so easy, but it isn't the truth, you've just admitted that's not the truth...

INGRID: Oh, fucking hell. We can't discuss these things. I was a young mum.

Tom is showing concern for you but for justified reasons, you don't want to accept that it is a genuine expression of his concern...

INGRID: I have always been like that... I always have to prove myself all the time, he's always digging for something all the time, it's always my dad but dad wasn't with me ever in my life. Never ever.

(Tom and Ingrid argue about Ingrid waking at night)

It's going to be very difficult if either one of you shows concern for the other, and that's...

INGRID: *(interrupts)* But I don't think he is concerned about me. If you were worried, you would hug me and say... you would be totally different, you wouldn't be like this...

TOM: I don't do badly.

INGRID: When you argue you say there must be something wrong with me. I know you so well.

TOM: I can't raise these issues without a screaming match. I have to tread carefully around you. You're volatile when you argue.

One of the things that Gillian and Penny did say was about

projection. It works both ways. When Tom says there must be something wrong with you to behave like that – is he expressing something about himself as well? But also when you say to him why are you digging about like this – are you also concerned that there's something to find in Tom's life?

INGRID: But there's nothing to find.

I'm not saying there is or there isn't – I'm saying because you're defensive.

INGRID: We've been together seven years. Tom didn't take responsibility for caring for us in all those years.

But as long as you hold on to that, all you're doing is revealing your weakness.

INGRID: Yes, I understand that. I'm weak

Not that you are weak, that's a very different thing. You are more concerned about – and we could say the same thing about Tom too – you are more concerned to hold on to what Tom didn't do for seven years than to move on.

INGRID: That's right, yes. Because I'm grieving about those things.

But at some point you have to make the decision to let go.

INGRID: Yes, I know.

Likewise Tom, you can't constantly say because Ingrid is volatile you can't communicate with her...

TOM: That's right.

(Tom and Ingrid both talk over each other)

Seeing you both together now, you might as well be in different rooms because you're not actually listening to each other at all. It's not just you, it's many couples in this situation.

INGRID: I know, I know.

(Yvonne asks Ingrid and Tom to discuss the issue of confidentiality.)

TOM: Ingrid, I respect your right to have your opinion. I hope you respect my right. We agreed we wouldn't have counselling in the first place. Obviously there are things we both don't understand and we've got to accept that there will be massive differences in what we've said [in interviews] but I can tell you... You can write exactly what you want about me...

INGRID: I know but when I read what you've said, if there's one thing that isn't true – fuck off! I want to see what you think about everything. What you think about love – I don't care what you say about me but I want to see what you say ... because if I read the book and it's untrue, then it's too late.

(Ingrid and Tom talk over each other)

TOM: Okay, I'll cut to the chase. I see a sadistic streak when it comes to Dan that I don't like. I don't want that sadistic streak to affect him That's how I see it. We should protect Dan.

INGRID: That's fine I agree.

TOM: Quite obviously, I'm getting angry from my point of view. You have your reasons and I have mine...

INGRID: *(sarcastically)* I can laugh, you were never here for Dan.

TOM: *(angry)* Let's get on with it. okay Ingrid? I could go into loads of things...

Let's just finish this discussion about confidentiality.

TOM: Ingrid has already told her mum and her sister [about the book]. She's trying to back track now and say she hasn't.

You said to me, your mum knows all about the book.

INGRID: Never ever. I'm not worried about [Tom's parents reading the book]. I'm worried about me reading the book and it's not true.

TOM: But your half of the book is going to be true to you isn't it? And my half is going to be true to me. I don't mind what you've written, I'll deal with it.

INGRID: I want everything to be perfect – I want it to be right.

Ingrid, you've just said you want everything to be perfect but there's no such thing... What is coming over strongly is that the book is becoming bigger than actually getting your relationship back on track . It should be the other way around.

TOM: I don't see it like that.

We can stop this because right from the beginning we said that if any of us felt it was doing more harm than good, then there was no point in continuing. This book isn't about your respective life stories. Hopefully, it's about improving the health of your relationship. I don't think either of you is doing any homework. It feels right now as if we're back where we were four months ago. You're both going on about the first seven years.

(Tom and Ingrid talk over each other)

INGRID: Tom, you have to change.

But as long as you constantly....

TOM: *(interrupts sarcastically)* It's got to be perfect.

INGRID: Not perfect but now, again, you've another job that's 24/7 – that's not fair.

What would you prefer?

INGRID: He's doing the same thing all the time...

185

But you said [before] that you felt that this was worthwhile, if financially it means that you were in a better place.

INGRID: I don't mind that he's working now so much – but he still leaves the kitchen like a bomb.

(To Tom) **Okay, so there's something practical. Can you talk to each other about that? I don't know if you do or don't but if you do, why do you leave it like a bomb?**

TOM: Okay, I can do more but I'm not sleeping well. And I'm just not that happy. I don't see any hope at the moment.

INGRID: Yes, that's right, you have the problem, You're telling me that I have the problem.

Why does that mean you leave it like a bomb?

TOM: I just feel like I'm rushing to get out of the house. I know I could do more but...

A lot of research into relationships shows that it's the incremental things. The tiny efforts you make to show you care.

INGRID: The tiny things if they happened would work a miracle in our relationship. If he did a little bit, if he came home and washed the dishes.

TOM: But we had a cleaner that I was paying for before...

Okay if you think about it in the longer run, what does it matter who is right, if you each say to the other, you are absolutely right. You could change the atmosphere between you. "You're absolutely right. I don't do enough in the house. I do leave it like bomb. I am going to make a difference..."

TOM: With Ingrid, " like a bomb" basically means that I didn't put a plate away.

Fine...Well that's not much to put away then is it? That's something simple. If Tom does make an effort, it's not a good

idea to keep going on about the first seven years.

INGRID: If he did those things I would be happy. He hates me because I'm not like his mum...

But how do you know he hates you?

INGRID: I just feel it. He tells me that his mum did everything. She never complains, I'm not a proper woman. You see me as some sort of feminist or something – yes you do, Tom.

TOM: I don't understand why you would consider yourself a feminist.

INGRID: Once we were in your house and your sister had made dinner and she said, "okay, it's somebody else's turn now I've finished. I've done my bit." Oh my God! – her husband helped with the washing up.

You think Tom hates you Ingrid. If Tom hates you why don't you talk about it?

TOM: Well, we don't really talk. It's not talking as such... I thought we we were making some progress – then it's drunken screaming in front of Dan, six or seven glasses of wine, three brandies.

INGRID: It was Sunday dinner with wine.

(Both talk angrily at the same time.)

It's very common if people are upset and unhappy that they have a drink and it does boil over. But remember what Penny and Gillian said about Dan. It's really, really important...

TOM: I see it as abuse really. Screaming in front of Dan

INGRID: Ninety per cent of the time I shout and scream, is when I'm telling you not to shout and scream. You're always having a go at me. Bloody hell, you get angry. Dan and I will leave and go to Scandinavia. You don't understand a fucking thing. *(Getting up)* I get really angry when you don't understand... *(Ingrid goes out)*

TOM: I think there's progress and then something happens and I just withdraw to be honest...

But do you think we should stop this and you perhaps both go to counselling separately?

TOM: I'm open to suggestions. I really am... I think you picked a good subject in us...

(Ingrid comes back) No time to see us Tom, never, ever. You never say to your mum, "Can you take Dan?". Never *(Ingrid goes out again; she says she is too angry to sit down; then comes back)*

INGRID: Wake up, Tom! I'm a human being... you say about your mother ironing your shirts and stuff.

TOM: I'm not impotent. I'm absolutely not interested in sex, right?

INGRID: You ask your mum to have Dan for you [to go out] but never for us.

TOM: It's just not true, is it?

What Ingrid is saying, isn't she, is that she wants time with you, not just to go out with her girl friends...

TOM: I find it difficult to spend time with you.

INGRID: You've never tried.

TOM: Ingrid that's a ridiculous statement. Do you think I've never tried?

INGRID: I can't talk to my mum or anyone because they'd say, "Why the hell are you with him anymore?" I ask myself why am I here? It's unbelievable. I'm so angry... I have to leave. *(Ingrid goes out of their room)*

TOM: Oh come and sit down, Ingrid.

INGRID: *(upset from the kitchen)* If I could speak to people about what you have done. You have to take some responsibility. I'm an easy-going person. I am not evil. You are evil. You are really.

(Ingrid returns, distressed, and apologises to Yvonne)

No, please you don't have to apologise. It's very painful for you...

INGRID: We are so different. He doesn't see these things. His family – Okay it's not his fault. It's his family's fault because they are from a different century but we aren't in that century any more.

That's the way Tom's family operates, you think?

INGRID: Yes, obviously. They told him, you stay in his old job. You don't go anywhere else, blah, blah, blah. I said leave the bloody job.

The question you have to ask yourself is whether you can get over that and move on...

INGRID: That's right. That's why I want to see what he's said. I just want to know what he thinks. The problems will be clearer.

Why does it matter what he thinks of you because he's going to be saying things because he's hurt? Can you stop seeing the person who hurt you and actually look for something more constructive in him?

INGRID: I can, yes I can.

You can? You can still see in Tom someone you'd want to stay with? And continue the relationship?

INGRID: Yes but I want him to grow up. It's not a man's world.

189

His family is so old fashioned. It's really difficult. Don't go to watch football on a Saturday night. He makes so many promises... and then he doesn't do it...

At some point you've got to say, what am I prepared to do to make this relationship work? Both of you...

INGRID: *(to Tom)* You're quite similar to your mum in one way...

TOM: I haven't got this big umbilical chord wrapped around my neck, whoever thinks that... it's laughable...

INGRID: You're a mummy's boy... worrying about mum, never worrying about me, walking her home...

(Both Ingrid and Tom talk over each other.)

TOM: You said things about my mum that were rather disgusting...

INGRID: Why didn't you buy me a Valentine's present? I have to tell you to do these things – book a restaurant – but you buy your mum flowers...

TOM: Why should I buy a Valentine present after what you said before? Those presents mean nothing. Why do you want some material gesture that means nothing to me? It's bloody rubbish that just because it's the "right" time of the year...

What do you think Ingrid is really saying when she's talking like that Tom? What do you think she's actually saying when she says you buy your mum a bunch of flowers. This is what Gillian and Penny are trying to encourage you to do.

TOM: If I did buy anyone else a present it's not about who's got the biggest one, is it really? My mum's not screaming and shouting.

INGRID: I've only been shouting in the last three months...

TOM: Only in the last three months? Since Dan was a year old...

INGRID: I haven't been shouting.

Ingrid, are you saying to Tom that you think he doesn't express enough affection for you?

TOM: The fact that Ingrid is saying that is ironic because that's what I've been asking for since she came here.

(Yvonne to Tom) **You married Ingrid knowing that she had difficulty expressing affection...**

TOM: I didn't know it would last forever.

INGRID: Now he's punishing me.

TOM: I'm not punishing you... it's self-defence, that's all it is.

INGRID: That's why I want to read what you've written... I want to know what you really think about me, my shouting...

Anyone shouting is a problem for a child. Gillian and Penny say that unless you look at your own behaviour and not the other person's – but still each of you are saying he said this and she said that – I don't know where we go from here...

TOM: I must admit, it would be very productive and positive if I could do that but I find it incredibly difficult to sit here and listen to things that I know in my heart are wrong. It's easy to say we have to think differently – but it is bloody difficult.

It is difficult.

INGRID: We haven't been doing our homework or anything. When I read that first report [from Gillian and Penny] I thought, "Okay, Okay, now I think we're getting somewhere..."

But it's no good reading their reports and then forgetting about them and continuing the arguments. Tom, I know it's difficult but it isn't going to be resolved.

INGRID: We don't argue like this all the time. But so many things have happened to us, unlucky things.

What do you mean by unlucky things? One of the things you have to say to yourself is am I part of the problem? If I leave, will something similar start happening again in another relationship?

TOM: We're both guilty of it – Ingrid has the seven years thing. I have her shouting thing.

Ingrid is also saying you treat home like a hotel... rightly or wrongly. You're both looking for gestures that you are cared for and wanted, and although Ingrid may talk about sex, isn't it also the intimacy that she may be missing?

INGRID: When I first came here I felt , "Aaah I've left my life, my job, I left everything..." I was a fucking stranger here and I was depressed about my jobs, selling bloody silly underwear. *(Both talk angrily over each other)*

Sometimes when a person falls in love, they withdraw because they don't like the feeling of being so vulnerable. They might not do it consciously but they will construct a life for themselves that reduces that sense of vulnerability.

INGRID: Another person might have said good-bye after one year.

TOM: When you came here the first thing you said was I'm not going to work for six months.

INGRID: I couldn't get a job for three months. Do you know what I put myself through? He's lying.

(Each interrupts the other.)

Ingrid, no matter how often you tell Tom he's lying, it's not going to change anything. You're both like hamsters in a wheel going round and round.

TOM: I didn't take a penny off you for anything, so I was in the same position whether you were working or not. I had to work extra hours. I had job opportunities. I had the chance of spending three months in Bournemouth on a course leading to the chance of a fantastic job and you wouldn't even let me do that. Do you remember the council house? You wouldn't live in a council house.

INGRID: That's right, I didn't want to live in one

TOM: Okay these are the things that I had to find solutions to.

INGRID: *(mocking)* You were so boyish, so babyish... I don't believe anything you say....

TOM: *(angry)* Okay, will you shut up and let me finish? It wasn't easy to earn enough for me and for you as well. You must realise that you didn't exactly help the situation.

INGRID: Okay, fine.

TOM: I'm really pissed off that you're just sitting there smiling and taking the piss. You're immature whether you like it or not, you really are. You didn't like it that your husband was a blue-collar worker. It didn't matter that I was doing something good, it didn't matter to you. You came to a pub, I remember, with your friend when you first arrived and looked at my uniform [in his previous job] and made some disgusting comments...

INGRID: Don't be so silly, so absurd.

TOM: It wasn't absurd, you were belittling me all the time. I had to tell your friends I was doing a different job. I wasn't important enough according to you because I didn't have a six figure salary.

Each of you not only wants to be right about those early years, you want the other person to say that you're right when they have their own version. The only reason for discussing the past is if something constructive is going to emerge. What we have to decide tonight is whether we should stop, whether you want counselling separately, whether you should think about splitting up or whether we continue to meet together or separately.

INGRID: I don't want to meet separately. I like to speak and be listened to because we don't do that at home... I'd like to know what he thinks...

TOM: I definitely saw an improvement, Ingrid, especially January and February. Okay, there's been relapses sometimes, terrible ones, but, for instance, I haven't been out nearly as much. Sometimes I think you're just trying to derail the whole thing. You keep saying seven years, seven years. In seven years' time, Ingrid, we'll be split up. This must be the last time we hear seven years and I'll do something in return. Whatever it takes. We've got to keep going for Dan Is it possible?

INGRID: Even now, I know this is just a game that Tom's playng... he' not really doing this...

Don't worry about what Tom is doing The point is that you look at your own behaviour and Tom looks at his. *(To Tom)* **You can't have it all ways; if it's only a plate that needs putting**

away, put the plate away; if a bunch of flowers once a week makes a difference, it's only a bunch of flowers. It's a gesture...

TOM: *(breaking in)* Not if it's in the wrong colour – if I buy the wrong colour then...

INGRID: That's right. You buy flowers. I think, Okay, why is he buying flowers?

But how is anything going to change if... What about the courtesies and pleasures of your life – I mean one of the things that Gillian and Penny said was that your lives seem very frenetic?

TOM: There's so much tension.

INGRID: We're never together at the same time at home...*(distressed)* I gave you the best years of my life, I still can't believe that....

The present could be the best years. Tom is 35, you're 40. It can be a very cold place, out there and single. You know each other well – I can still see you've got affection between you – dimly.

(Tom laughs; Ingrid smiles)

You have a little boy who's gorgeous. Being "right" is the most worthless element in any relationship

TOM: It's also the most difficult thing to ignore.

It is the most difficult thing but at some point you have to say, are we really going to make a go of this?

TOM: We need a truce because she has her version of the truth and I have my version.

Well, it's not even versions of the truth. They are both defence mechanisms that help you to survive after a fashion in the relationship. You might think it's the "truth" but sometimes

Gillian and Penny can see a different set of explanations, different patterns. I think they are trying to say, one day you may be able to recognise these patterns yourselves.

INGRID: I cook sometimes and he says he hates my cooking. We don't ever eat together.

TOM: What? I am shocked you said that. You don't cook, you never cook. You put it on a plate and leave it on the stove.

INGRID: It's no point in doing anything for you... you're never here.

TOM: I can count a few times when she came home and made me dinner.

INGRID: Well, you never cook for me.

You have a choice here. Are you going to continue a war of attrition in which you each give the other more reasons to separate, or are you going to grow up and say for Dan's sake – if that has to be the excuse – we're going to do something about it? To be honest, any fool can make life uncomfortable for another person. The hardest thing is making it nice – small things like offering to cook dinner.

INGRID: How many times have you done that Tom?

TOM: It's not the fact you cook dinner, it's the fact that you say, "You want it, you take it. It's in the oven..."

INGRID: Did I? Did I? Have I said those things? You are a liar, liar, liar *(very agitated)*.

(Ingrid and Tom shout at each other.)

Hold on, hold on. Never mind who cooks what. The whole point about having a meal is that you sit down together to eat.

INGRID: That's right. That never happens. I hate it, I really hate *it*.

(Both shout at the same time – incoherent.)

TOM: I can see it's a bloody difficult undertaking to get you off the last seven years. I'm not going to go on about what I think you've done in front of Dan... The point is...

INGRID: So what have *you* done in front of Dan, Tom?

TOM: I've done terrible things.

INGRID: *(distressed)* He hit me, he hit me... Have you told her?

TOM: You can tell her anything... you've hit me dozens of times. I've never hit you. I might have kicked you up the arse a couple of times... When Dan was asleep, you were screaming and I had to throw you into the bedroom... *(Ingrid talking over Tom – difficult to decipher)* You've punched me and kicked me and I've never responded. If you're such a feminist as you say you are. I can't lose my...

INGRID: When I was pregnant... it was too much. I asked him to move a nappy table from the living-room to the bedroom. It was too much – I waited months, then I did it myself and you punched me...

TOM: *(very angry and agitated)* Punched you? Punched you?

INGRID: The whole thing...

TOM: Have I ever punched you in my life? Punched you! That's a complete bloody lie. On Dan's life, I've never done that...

INGRID: In the face.

TOM: When did I punch you in the face? You were scratching my face and I pushed you into the wall. Did I punch you in the face?

INGRID: *(smiling)* Yes, you did.

TOM: *(very cross)* Keep saying yes – did I punch you in the face

197

or did I push you off me? Tell me I punched you in the face. Tell the truth!

INGRID: Tom!

TOM: You're a bloody liar. When did I punch you? Or were you scratching my face off? I've never punched you in my life… you were scratching my face to pieces, what did you expect me to do, stand there? Did you scratch my face? Did I have make-up on my face for about a bloody month?

INGRID: Yes I did.

TOM: Am I entitled to push you away? I think I am. Don't tell me I punched you.

INGRID: *(defiantly shouting)* What did you do then?

TOM: I pushed you into a bloody wall. I've never closed my fist to you in my life. Did I punch you? Tell me what I did?

INGRID: I could've killed you many times. Something's changed now…

TOM: I've never punched you in my life and you've punched me over 500 times and don't ever say during this relationship that you… Did I punch you?

INGRID: Yes, you did . You did, you did.

TOM: Show me how I punched you.

(Ingrid suddenly jumps out of her armchair and aggressively pushes the flat of her hand hard into Tom's face and then leaves the room)

TOM: *(very distressed, shouting)* I'm so pissed off with you bloody lying. You can't tell the truth. *(Ingrid comes back into the room)* Tell me did I punch you? Look at you enjoying your bloody self. Did I close my fist and punch you?

INGRID: *(outside the sitting-room)* No.

TOM: Did I or did I not? Fucking simple.

Tom, Ingrid has said no.

TOM: *(shouting)* Yes or no! Tell me what I did.

She did tell you Tom.

TOM: You enjoy conflict, you can't just tell the truth. You can't bloody answer the question...

Tom... Ingrid wants you to be angry...

TOM: She's lying and that bloody does make me angry. I pushed you away with all my force. You had your bloody nails to my face.

INGRID: I was pushed into the bedroom.

TOM: Because you were abusing Dan, you were abusing him nonstop.

INGRID: Stop it Tom. What are you saying...

TOM: No taboos, no. I have to admit, I get angry. You've punched me in the face hundreds of times. Did I curl up when you punched me around the head? Did I curl up with my face bleeding and bruised? I drove one hundred miles to get away from you.

INGRID: He came after me like a mad man into the toilet...

TOM: It's abuse, screaming at Dan for little things...

INGRID: Disgusting man.

TOM: I've barricaded the door against her 50 times because you're drunk and screaming out of your mind... one inch from Dan's room

INGRID: *(distressed)* I'll go, I'll go back to Scandinavia.

TOM: If you leave I don't want you to to take Dan. I don't think you're a fit mother...

INGRID: He's trying to drive me mad

TOM: I'd phone you from work and you'd be screaming at Dan. And I'm not hearing it again, ever – not in front of Dan, never. I'm not hearing it now, tomorrow or next week Never! *(very angry)*

INGRID: It's not true! How did I get my whole face black?

TOM: I pushed your face into the wall – everything was self-defence. You're not listening to me or Penny or Gillian or anyone... You're screaming in front of Dan every night.

INGRID: You are lying... You've got the problem with anger.

TOM: You've got a problem with anger

INGRID: I've never hit anybody ever.

TOM: You can't say you haven't hit anyone – you've hit loads of people.

INGRID: I've never hit anybody ever, you fucking disgusting man. That's so disgusting. I feel so bad – I can't do anything with you, you just make me feel really evil.

TOM: Yvonne, I'm incredibly sorry but I'm glad you saw it... that's the reality.

(Ingrid walks out)

You don't have to apologise but my main concern is what's best to do... I'm worried that you'll hurt each other seriously...

(Ingrid comes back into the room upset and angry)

INGRID: Don't lie. You say I scream in front of Dan.

TOM: You do, you do.

(Each talks over the other)

Do you agree that there's too much shouting in front of Dan? You said things had improved in front of him.

TOM: Yes, they had.

Because he really, really will start to suffer if this goes on...

200

TOM: Do you understand that, Ingrid?

But both of you, the way you behave, you ...

INGRID: *(interrupts)* You're absurd, and you make me so mad... How many times have you kicked the door?

Maybe you each need to go to anger management or counselling?

TOM: I don't want Dan with her – If you leave I don't want you to have Dan... I'll do anything to protect him – I'm not making excuses about me being a bad father.

INGRID: You've never been at home, Tom. Sorry. You're a liar, I don't care what you think...

TOM: You've just proved you're a liar – you said something about me punching you and then you retracted it.

INGRID: You did – that's why I want to see what's written down... I always have to prove myself...

Why do you have to prove yourself? Why do you imagine people are going to believe what Tom says rather than what you say?

INGRID: Because I feel so horrible with him. I feel he is so like Hitler. I feel so bad at the moment... I give up!

TOM: *(angry)* Don't give up on Dan, Ingrid, give up on me but not on Dan. You don't deserve him.

Hang on, you're both parents, so you both deserve Dan and more to the point, he deserves you both in a happier situation..

TOM: Not like this he doesn't. I'd rather he never saw me and he was happy.

INGRID: Dan is coming with me. I know I am going to my mum's.

TOM: A good mum wouldn't behave like that in front of him. Sorry. I think it's perfectly justifiable to say that that is abuse. You don't understand that, you think it's fine.

You're both doing the same thing again. Ingrid is behaving as she is because she's getting triggers from you.

TOM: Yes she is – she's winding me up. She knows damn well I'd never punch her – she's milking it and letting me get angry.

Hold on, let's go back to square one – violence is unacceptable.

INGRID: I want to read what he's written.

You're both going to see everything before it's published anyway – the issue is not the book – it's whether you want to stay together and sure as shite you're not making much effort. You are behaving like two children in the playground. I understand it's easy for me to say that but I need to talk to Gillian and Penny because you both have such anger... It's frightening to see, and it's definitely not the best way to heal a relationship, is it ?

INGRID: No.

You have to decide. One, do you want to carry on with this. Two, do you want to stop and go to counselling. It is quite normal for a relationship to get rocky before it gets better because things are changing. That's what Gillian and Penny have said.

TOM: That's why I'm hoping it will get better – you have to take comfort from small things – I want you to say shouting is not acceptable.

INGRID: okay then.

TOM: But you can't do it, Ingrid.

But then you Tom make the small gestures, too.

TOM: I will, I will. If it means buying a Valentine's present, forget it because...

INGRID: How can I think about doing anything with him?

Okay, why are you even trying?

INGRID: I've got nowhere else to go.

That's not true.

INGRID: I know. I'm not ready. I don't know. I think if I leave now...

But you can also say, you've got a commitment to the relationship, that's all right, too.

INGRID: I have.

You have got a commitment?

INGRID: Yes. I don't know what to think. I know what it would cost Tom and his parents if I took Dan. I have to think about everyone else, not me...

You're doing what Gillian and Penny picked up on earlier – living your life through Tom. In the long run, it's not good for you or Dan. It's not great for a child to have his parents split up but if you're going to stay together. I know it is difficult...

INGRID: We're not arguing every day.

TOM: I believe that

INGRID: Dan's happy. We're not normal but we have to sort this out.

But "normal" from what you're telling me isn't what some couples call normal. Two of you seem to be living side by side, not together. There's so much resentment on both sides – you can let that fester, in which case you haven't a hope of staying

together happily, or you start doing something about it. The doing something about it may not be this book. It might mean you get orthodox counselling. Whatever it is, it will be painful. You can't keep imagining the most important thing is to be right. For Dan's sake and your own – it's one of the hardest things anyone ever does to try and turn a relationship around. But they do do it. Not now, but perhaps later, if there's a reasonable moment, to talk to each other about this anger but don't just talk, listen. Neither of you listens. Ingrid told you, Tom, that you hadn't punched her but it was important for your reputation, so you kept repeating yourself. You wanted Ingrid to say you hadn't punched her as if she was in a court of law.

TOM: Yes. She was playing the situation. It was so important to me. You could've said, "I didn't punch you, I pushed you into the wall."

It doesn't matter who did what to whom – what does matter is that there is violence between you.

TOM: I've got to defend myself

INGRID: Defend yourself?

Neither of you should be using violence. Neither of you

TOM: When you walk out of the room I get a punch or a flick on the head or something – I don't do that to you.

INGRID: I don't recognise myself sometimes. He makes me feel evil.

TOM: No, you're not evil.

INGRID: You make me feel really bad.

TOM: I haven't got this angry for a year but this has really struck a chord with me.

INGRID: Fucking hell, you kicked me into the bedroom.

TOM: I've never heard my mum and dad have one row in forty years. We lived in a small house; not one row so don't start on about my family. I've never had a family swearing and shouting, I'm not used to it. Every time we have a row, it's something incredible.

INGRID: When we were teenagers we had arguments but not like this.

TOM: Why are you doing it in front of Dan then?

INGRID: Because of you – how can I explain it to you? **Relationships aren't just isolated things on their own. They are plugged into childhood. Nobody makes someone evil. In a relationship, a whole lot of buttons are pressed. Each partner learns how to bring out the best and the worst in the other. One partner's "bad" behaviour can be manipulated and provoked by the ostensibly "innocent" partner and vice versa. Anger is often a mixture of loving and hating and children are in the middle. I need to talk to Gillian and Penny about this. Maybe you'd be better off going to counselling – if you'd go?**

INGRID: I don't trust counselling. Sorry.

TOM: I'm committed to this – to do whatever it takes. **It would be good if you could calm down even if it means not talking to each other for the rest of the evening. In some ways it has been constructive – different layers of anger and frustration have sort of peeled away. And you both have a desire to do what's best for Dan. It's a lot to think about.**

***

The following day, Tom sent an e-mail:

> I am totally numb. The rest of the evening was silent after you went. I am losing the will to fight for my marriage and Dan. I do not know what to do for the best. I am so sorry you had to witness what happened between me and Ingrid but it was an insight into the sad truth of our relationship. Everything is really bad at the moment and I regret that you saw me at my worst when I should have been at my best. I think I should have anger management if it helps Dan, Ingrid should as well.
>
> I have tried harder with the little things but I have problems giving those little things to Ingrid. It is a catch-22. I have to learn to break the concrete cycle I've helped to create. Ingrid has tried to speak to me but I do not know what to say any more. I am feeling so low about every aspect of my life right now. I just feel like crying all the time. Please do not give up on us. This is going to be very difficult but hopefully worthwhile.

Ingrid also sent an e-mail:

> It was good to see you and good to talk!! Sorry we lost our temper (me too emotional, emotions – for both of us – seem to build up) I have not spoken about that "incident" to anybody and somehow it was a relief to bring it up. I take responsibility for my part in that. Anyway, I think we are going somewhere by talking about these painful things together. Certainly

I have not given up and lost my hope about staying together. This is the only way for me, and divorcing is not what I want, it would not be good for us...

Ingrid and Dan then left for a week's Easter holiday in Scandinavia. I seriously considered stopping the whole process because of the anger and aggression both Ingrid and Tom had displayed. I liked both of them, but on that evening, their hostility towards each other was ugly to witness. They had pulled back as presumably they had not done on other occasions. It was also becoming clearer that Tom, too, contributed to the pattern of shouting that Dan was witnessing – and, while Ingrid might be volatile, he also had a temper initially camouflaged by his affability. My obvious concern was that the process of interviewing was doing more harm than good.

CHAPTER TWENTY

April: Gillian and Penny's fifth response

Immediately after the evening with Tom and Ingrid I emailed Gillian and Penny and we arranged to bring our meeting forward. Our conversation was longer than usual because of the threat of violence that I'd witnessed and the evidence that both Ingrid and Tom had been physically aggressive towards each other at times. How should we respond? Might our interventions make violence more likely rather than less?

***

The violence displayed by both Ingrid and Tom is a very, very serious concern. Alternative ways of dealing with anger and frustration *have* to be found, not least because once violence is present in a relationship it frequently escalates. It is a very dangerous path to take. The argument exposes a pattern – each time Ingrid and Tom come to a point of agreement in which they can glimpse they have shared issues, they pull away and start arguing again about those first seven years.

Tom was very upset by Ingrid's criticism of his father but perhaps he might consider that Ingrid was retaliating because Tom often, by innuendo, refers to her father and something that may or may not have happened in her past. He appears to be saying, "Look what he did to you, and that's why you behave as you do..." Ingrid is saying, "Now you know what it feels like..."

Is it possible that when Ingrid was very young, she witnessed her own parents arguing in a very volatile way? This may be the cause of her waking, up calling for her mother? (This may also tell Ingrid and Tom something about the long-term impact of arguing in front of Dan.) It may also explain why anger and the expression of anger has never been made safe for her. Anger is frightening both to witness and to experience – especially because of the fear of what the angry person might do to someone else. For example, when a small child has a tantrum, one of the best and most loving ways of handling it is to hold him or her so the infant feels safe and protected from herself. For Ingrid, perhaps, the combination of feeling as if, no matter what she says, she isn't "heard" by Tom and the erroneous belief that any expression of anger is "bad", adds to the tensions the relationship. What matters is not continuing to press each other's buttons in a destructive way – but understanding each other. Psychological warfare and one-upmanship obviously does not help.

Low self-esteem may be an issue for both Ingrid and Tom.

If an individual lacks a strong sense of self, they may fall in love with a person whom, superficially, appears to be a reflection of themselves – but in a more perfect form. They also project on to the other person virtues they wish they had. If there is low self-esteem, a person may subconsciously believe that nobody could possibly love them – so they feel terrifically energised when they do meet "the one" – who is allegedly a reflection of their better self. Each person in the partnership eventually develops a more realistic view of the other. In doing so, they have to let go of the fantasy of a relationship that never was and could never be. Losing the fantasy is painful so each blames the other for the destruction of that dream. Inevitably, as this unfolds, there is both anger and disappointment. The pull of the fantasy is so strong, each person believes that the only change needed to make things better is for the other person to become what they appeared to be at the outset of the relationship. As a result, they don't see the need to change themselves.

This is perhaps why it's proving so hard to move on from the first seven years. During the argument, Ingrid and Tom, hopefully, reached a major turning point – they took a risk and revealed their less than perfect selves to an outsider. This may provide the opportunity to manage their own feelings better – to listen to each other – and then to understand what it is each person is hearing and saying and why. As the argument illustrated repeatedly, what Ingrid and Tom hear isn't necessarily what the other person is actually saying. If both Ingrid and Tom can explore their own childhoods realistically, that may also have a positive impact on how they parent

Dan. Tom has made several references to depression – perhaps he needs to pay serious attention to why he suffers from depression and how it might be tackled. Drinking alcohol is also a way of self-soothing – of dulling the pain – but also it gives the (false) courage to say what is too risky to say sober. (False because not much can be remembered the following day.)

The issue of anonymity in the book is very important – for Dan's sake but also to preserve Tom and Ingrid's privacy and future relationship. The important element is not the book – it is trying to improve a relationship in a way that, hopefully, helps Ingrid and Tom to stop the destruction and build a healthier and more loving partnership. It may also provide some insight for other couples who are reluctant to seek counselling but who can see their own reflections in the way Ingrid and Tom behave towards each other – and be encouraged by the changes that, hopefully, Ingrid and Tom will eventually make.

CHAPTER TWENTY-ONE
Intimate terrorism

The young woman was 22 with a new born baby and a two year old. She had the baby in her arms and she was distraught. She had fled her home after her boyfriend had physically attacked her for the umpteenth time – but she'd been unable to taker her older son, sleeping on the sofa.

I was writing a feature on one of the first women's refuge for the *Sunday Times*. It was almost 30 years ago when help for survivors of domestic violence and their children was virtually non-existent. This refuge, in the south of England, struggled month by month for funds. Women and children were crammed in every available room. What shocked me was her injuries. Her legs, back and arms were the colour of rotten bananas. She had a split lip, a black eye and a cut on the back of her head. She had been beaten, she said, because she had been late in producing her boyfriend's tea. All she could think of was her son.

The refuge manager was an inspirational and charismatic

woman, herself once a battered wife and mother of five, who had been free of her abusive husband and working in the refuge for a couple of years. She said there was little point in calling the police. (Today, as a result of the Domestic Violence Crime and Victims Act 2004, and a number of Home Office initiatives, it ought to be different.) The refuge manager and I drove the young woman to her home on a pleasant private housing estate. As soon as we turned into her cul-de-sac, she began to shake. She was too terrified to leave the car. The manager and I went to the front door. A man in his early thirties answered the door, saw his girlfriend in the car and slammed it shut again, but not before cursing and threatening to give us, "More of what that bitch has had." We could hear the child crying indoors.

The following morning, a social worker and policeman successfully rescued the toddler who was tearful but unharmed. The mother had been beside herself because the boyfriend was not the father and he had hit the child on occasions before. A day later, in a cafe in the town, a woman in her late twenties was sitting with her ex-boyfriend and two of us from the refuge. He had asked to meet us to hand over some of her property. She insisted on neutral ground, with us as support. Three minutes after we'd all cautiously sat down, without warning, he clenched his fist and hit her hard on the side of her jaw, sending her backwards in her chair. That, he said, was for leaving. She refused to allow us to call the police.

Domestic violence is a hygienic phrase which encompasses physical, emotional, sexual and psychological abuse. It is about one person attempting to control the actions, thoughts

213

and behaviour of another to an extreme degree. It may mean, for instance, that a woman is kept short of money and her life and the lives of her children are horrendously restricted. It may mean that a woman or a man is so constantly criticised, mocked and undermined, that they lose much of their sense of self and their will to fight back drains away.

Domestic violence is chronically under-reported but it is estimated that it accounted for 16 per cent of all violent crime in England and Wales in 2004/2005. On average, a person will have experienced 35 assaults before the police are contacted. It affects one in four women and one in six men over their life time, according to Home Office research. Two women a week are killed by a violent partner.

Violence is sporadically present in Ingrid and Tom's relationship – but it doesn't meet the criteria of domestic violence in which the man exercises abusive control and the aggression escalates over time. So what is going on? In the 1990s, the American sociologist Michael Johnson asked the question, "What are the roots of couple conflict and what is its consequence for individuals and couples?" He also controversially argued that an answer couldn't be given until there was a clearer distinction between the kinds of violence taking place in the home. He went on to distinguish between "patriarchal terrorism", inflicted mainly but not exclusively by men that is about systematic power and control – and "common couple conflict", also known as "intimate terrorism" (IT) which, he argued, has different roots and consequences but also draws on the dark and dangerous side of love, rooted in anxiety.

Commonly, in couple conflict, aggression is triggered by

specific situations and is less frequent. According to Johnson, patriarchal terrorism is 97 per cent male, escalates in three out of four cases and wives don't physically resist. In common couple violence, it s 56 per cent male, while women initiate the violence in 44 per cent of instances. It escalates in only one in four cases and women do physically resist.

British research published in 2003 supports Johnson's findings. The co-author, John Archer, professor of psychology at the University of Central Lancashire, also published a study three years earlier in which he analysed 82 US and UK studies on aggression dating back to the 1970s, an analysis of the behaviour of 34,000 men and women. He concluded that while men are far more likely to inflict serious injury on their partner, men also made up 40 per cent of the victims in the cases he'd studied. They had been the recipients of female aggression defined as pushing, slapping and hurling objects.

While power and control is at the root of patriarchal violence – common sense tells us that if we're witnessing more cases of female aggression on the streets, in pubs and from bullies in schools, there's no reason to doubt that it's also present in intimate relationships. It's also bound to have an effect on children who witness parents behaving aggressively towards each other. Home Office research says that psychological and behavioural problems are more common in children who have witnessed assaults in the family than in other children. The Children and Adoption Act (2000) states that witnessing violence is itself a form of emotional abuse. One or both people in a partnership may hit out because of frustration, anger and the growing realisation that a prolonged and fruitless attempt to resolve the conflict is turning to ashes. Each person plays a part in this dangerous game.One may strike the first blow, but the other, using sarcasm and verbal cruelty, also helps to create the moment.

In popular culture, the personal confession rules. Celebrities and lesser mortals tell the world their most intimate secrets, yet silence falls when it comes to a couple acting like bullies in the boudoir. On the rare occasion when the taboo is broken, as in the case of Rebekah Wade, editor of the *Sun,* and her husband, actor Ross Kemp, it's treated as adult entertainment. We teach children that lashing out is wrong – yet as grown-ups we endorse such behaviour by treating it as a joke. On the contrary, any kind of violence sounds a death knell for a healthy relationship.

CHAPTER TWENTY-TWO

May: Ingrid and Tom's sixth interview

As I drove to Tom and Ingrid's for our sixth interview, I experienced mixed emotions. We were more than halfway through the twelve months and Gillian and Penny had suggested that it was perhaps time to get a bit tougher.

In the previous couple of weeks, both Ingrid and Tom had e-mailed to say they were talking again and they were beginning to have a more constructive dialogue about their problems (at least by e-mail). Except, of course, they had reached this position a couple of times before, only to slip back into acrimony. After years of arguing, animosity was more comfortable for them than taking the risk of looking at themselves honestly in the mirror.

***

Shall we start? Nothing about the first seven years because I feel I know that intimately now.

(Ingrid and Tom laugh.)

TOM: We were better for a while and then a downturn again and now we're getting better again.

INGRID: A little bit better, yes, we have been e-mailing quite a lot.

When you're talking to each other by e-mail are you clarifying things or still going back to the first seven years?

TOM: I think that's always going to pop up. I'm just resigned to that now.

INGRID: We [go back] because we need to know why we are in the situation – why we are so on edge, why we are out of control.

When you say "we"?

INGRID: I mean I – I am – if I had been happy the last seven years I wouldn't be in this situation.

TOM: Can we talk about the positive things we've done?

INGRID: Can I just say why I think we are here?

According to Gillian and Penny, you have to do the equivalent of putting those last seven years in a little boat and let it drift towards the horizon. They suggested in their last response that the undertow [of your arguments] might be that something happened between you and your father?

(Ingrid interrupts)

I'm not saying it did. Gillian and Penny are suggesting – they are not saying it's true – they are suggesting that perhaps your parents might have argued [a great deal]?

INGRID: But they didn't even live together.

They might not have lived together but...

INGRID: He was abroad, he was never there. My mum, we

were three girls – we would argue when we feel something, we say it.

TOM: *(mocking)* No.

No. Okay, so why did your sister have therapy?

INGRID: After my mum divorced, it was very difficult for my sister. My father's parents actually told my mum's parents it's better they divorce – My mum was 24 or 25 or something – I feel sorry for her...

She didn't really want a divorce?

INGRID: I think the situation – he was always away.

TOM: Like me...

INGRID: It was a funny situation. My mum was on maternity leave and then she had to go back to work. It was a difficult time, she was going through the divorce... My mum never said anything to my sister like, our father was terrible. She didn't feel like that.

TOM: But you did say something to me about why you might shout in your sleep. It was the first time I'd heard that.

INGRID: We were at my grandparents house.

You stayed with your grandparents?

INGRID: After my mother's divorce we stayed there sometimes. My grandmother told me, I used to cry, "Mummy! Mummy!" Perhaps I was upset when she went to work.

TOM: Your mum left you when she went to work?

INGRID: *(exasperated)* Nobody left me – we had maternity leave of six months, do you understand? Nobody left me... My grandmother said "What are you doing?" I said I'm calling mum [when she was at work]. She said no you're not. I said yes I am.

TOM: You haven't done it for weeks [crying out in her sleep], you know. It must be about a month

INGRID: My sister told me she never thought I would suffer anything because I was the baby. I was lucky. I always went to my mum's bed to sleep I was always there. I used to be up at night – I didn't sleep much. I wanted to be with my mum and she was working in the day so I would be up at night.

You felt you were the one who got the attention?

INGRID: Yes, more or less.

Each one of you, Tom first and then Ingrid, what's changed and what hasn't changed?

TOM: It was obviously a bit traumatic. I remember what you said about "things have to come out". And that was the moment for Ingrid when something came out that was good [about missing her mother when she was working]. It might not be much to Ingrid but it was the first time I'd heard it and it was good. But what we've done as well, and Gillian and Penny might be interested, I said to my mum, "You're not going to wash my shirts anymore".

INGRID: I phoned, I told her.

TOM: Ingrid, be quiet! You don't get it do you? Ingrid may have said something to my mum as well but when I went round there, I said to my mum, "No, you're not doing it any more."

How did she react to that?

TOM: She said "Okay – look, anytime I can help, let me know." I said "fine but I don't think we will anymore." Now, I'm doing my own washing *(laughs)*.

INGRID: God! That's not what happened.

TOM: From my point of view that's what happened – you might have had conflict with my mum as well. But from my point of view that's what happened.

(Ingrid interrupts – talk over each other)

Hang on, don't get angry with each other – there's always more than one reality – it's not a game, it's not a competition for either of you. So what's happened that's positive?

TOM: Ingrid has agreed to drink just one or two glasses of wine.

INGRID: Oh my God! Agreed? What are you talking about? Who said about rules?

Hold on, you've made some rules?

INGRID: That's not the problem, Tom.

Hold on.

INGRID: *(angry)* Why are you saying those things Tom?

TOM: I'm trying to talk about the things we've agreed to do.

(Both talk over each other).

Shall I tell you what I think is happening?

TOM: *(to Ingrid)* You can't sit there and...

Maybe Ingrid feels very sensitive about...

TOM: Everything.

About how she thinks she's being portrayed. Actually, Tom isn't painting a picture of you. He's telling Gillian and Penny more about himself, whatever he says. It's not necessarily a reflection of the truth about you, Ingrid. It's much more constructive if you don't keep correcting him because...

INGRID: Okay. What they said in the last e-mail and what they said about my father, isn't true.

That's fine. Even what they are saying isn't "The Truth" – it's

a catalyst to help you both to think again about your own lives and how you interact. So Tom, are you saying you made some rules? Are those rules still applying?

TOM: We only started on Sunday.

INGRID: We've been e-mailing.

Sunday you made the rules but there's been quite a lot of time before that —what happened then?

TOM: Bad times – a lot of things came out – a lot of problems.

INGRID: We have arguments all the time.

So that's not very productive is it – what's it achieving?

TOM: Nothing.

It's using time and space and energy. I know it's easy for me to say as an outsider but the crux is that you can carry on having the same arguments and carry on living in the past, or are you going to make the next step?

TOM: We've done positive things. The washing is a big thing. I've said I'll only go out once a week. Ingrid says she's not going to drink more than one or two glasses with a meal.

INGRID: That is not the main problem.

(Ingrid and Tom talk over each other)

TOM: You're missing the point, Ingrid.

Hold on, Tom, you mustn't keep saying that because it's not constructive. Ingrid, what are you hearing when Tom says you've agreed to drink one or two glasses of wine? What actually are you hearing?

INGRID: I'm hearing, "How can he say that to me?" I don't drink at home. He goes out sometimes three times a week and he says to me you can't drink at home

What you are actually hearing is an accusation that you drink too much.

INGRID: Yes, that's right.

But it's not what he's saying – he's saying Ingrid has agreed to drink one or two glasses.

TOM: That's what you said in the e-mails, word for word.

I understand people press buttons and it's very difficult.

INGRID: I always understand him. He's looking like an angel now. It's my choice to have a glass or two of wine.

Nobody's saying it isn't.

INGRID: He's saying, I can't have a drink with dinner.

TOM: That's what you wrote.

INGRID: I did, I did.

TOM: So why are we arguing about this?

INGRID: Because I don't see that it's the problem.

Nobody's saying it's the problem. If anything it's a tribute to you – it says you're mature enough to say, "If that's what makes Tom happy, I'll agree". Both of you argue about something that was said eight or five years ago or whatever. That's the habit that has to get broken. Nobody is judging anyone on this. No one is saying, "Oh God, she must be an alcoholic, he must be a mummy's boy" – no one's saying that. What they are trying to say is, "What are the causes of conflict and how do you stop them?"

TOM: That's the positive way of looking at... I don't think that you can call me a mummy's boy when I say to my mum, don't wash my shirts.

INGRID: I think you're a mummy's boy anyway – that's not the thing.

TOM: Why are you being...

INGRID: Because we've gone through this so many times over the last two months, da, da, da, da...

TOM: You wrote something very good. You don't have to defend it.

INGRID: I'm not defending it.

TOM: You don't have to get angry about it.

INGRID: Somehow you're saying to me, I'm the one with the problem.

TOM: No, I've got my problems.

(Both talk over each other)

Hang on, why has it become a competition? Instead of worrying about the other person's behaviour, just worry about your own. I think this is an example of...

TOM: Not moving on – being stuck. This why we're stuck. I thought it was a really positive thing to do, now you're putting a negative spin on it.

INGRID: okay, I'm not.

TOM: That's exactly what you've done. I'm telling you something good and you want to see it in a bad way. It was a good thing...

INGRID: That's right, it was a good thing, Tom.

TOM: So don't look at it in another way...

Now you're not hearing what Ingrid's saying. She's saying, "yes it was a good thing." You're doing exactly the same thing she was doing fifteen minutes ago. She's saying "yes, it was a positive thing."

TOM: I'm saying, move on.

But you're not saying that. You have to listen to her as well.

224

It's like seeing a child in a supermarket The mother or father raises a hand and she flinches, expecting to defend herself. You two do that verbally.

INGRID: He has said so many times about the drinking but that's not the problem. It's about our relationship. Once, I have one or two drinks, I explode and he thinks that's the problem. I go to bed at 9 o'clock – I go to bed early and he stays here until midnight. We don't go out anywhere. We haven't been out for ever, for a very long time. He goes out alone.

TOM: So do you, Ingrid.

There you go again. I mean for God's sake. Don't be so defensive. You're provoking him, that's for sure. If you say, "We never go anywhere and, when he does, he wants to go alone," of course, it's like putting red meat into a lion's cage – so why say it?

INGRID: That's right, yes.

So, instead of saying it – decide you're not going to say it. Decide that tomorrow Dan is going to have a babysitter and you'll go out together – can you do that?

TOM: We could do that but I don't think we're quite...

Ingrid's saying yes and you're saying no.

TOM: She's hoping I'll say yes...

INGRID: I'm willing to go out any time but he's not willing to go anywhere.

I'm under orders from Gillian and Penny to get tough, so I'm going to get tough. Ingrid, Tom has to decide whether he's going to go out. It's not productive to say, "I'll go but he doesn't want to..." And Tom, you're sitting there saying "I'm

225

going to say yes because she thinks I'm going to say no..."

TOM: *(laughs)* I know she's saying no because she thinks... of course, I'll say yes.

Okay, so you're hearing now, he's saying yes. So are you going out tomorrow?

INGRID: You are already going out...

TOM: That's my once a week because the FA Cup Final is on but...

That's Saturday...

INGRID: That's what I mean, he can't leave early for me and Dan.

(Tom and Ingrid talk over each other)

All right, Ingrid, you're saying he can't leave work an hour earlier...

TOM: I don't take days off in the week, Ingrid.

Hold on Tom, is Ingrid saying she wants you to take a day off in the week?

TOM: No

What's she actually saying then?

TOM: About taking an hour off for her and Dan.

Listen to what's she saying. She didn't say "take the day off," she said "an hour earlier" – that doesn't seem unreasonable.

TOM: No it's not unreasonable. The reason I reacted is because she wants me to take days off not hours.

But that's not what she said.

INGRID: Sundays, bank holidays, Easter, he's always working.

Tom, Ingrid said she'd like you to take an hour, and you went into a thing about days off.

TOM: I appreciate that.

Gillian and Penny were asking why you both seem so frightened of change? Why not actually say, this Sunday I will come out of work an hour earlier? To be honest, you've got a family and Dan isn't going to stop growing up just because you're working flat out. He deserves some of your time too.

TOM: Of course, he comes to the office sometimes on Saturday and Sunday.

What Ingrid's saying is not that she begrudges you time off to go to football. What she's saying is the priority is football, not her and Dan. That seems to be a reasonable thing to say.

TOM: That seems to me to be reasonable too. I understand that. I've got no problem about taking time off to be with Ingrid and Dan.

Then that has to happen

TOM: What I'm saying is – I don't want to get into the habit of taking time off. We've been invited to weddings, Norfolk, Cambridge, Enfield. I said no to everything. I said no to going on Eurostar for a weekend. I'm working every day for myself and Dan and Ingrid. I told Ingrid that I hope by the end of the year that we can go to Scandinavia for a week over Xmas.

INGRID: *(exasperated)* I've already waited seven years... I won't believe it...

(Tom groans)

Ingrid, what is so terrible about you saying, "Okay, we're moving into a new phase" and give Tom the benefit of the doubt? He says you are going to Scandinavia for Christmas.

INGRID: Okay, I'm thinking in my head, maybe we'll go.

If you're looking forward to going isn't that going to have

a better result than saying, "Why should I believe you, it's never happened before when you've promised?" because you're angry about those seven years.

INGRID: That's right.

The anger isn't going to get you anywhere.

INGRID: I know, I know.

(to Tom) It's tough for Ingrid and Dan, you're working round the clock and they're not getting any...

TOM: I know, I know. Absolutely.

INGRID: That's what it was like for seven years you understand.

But you said two meetings ago that you could understand this now... Tom is working for himself so it's different isn't it?

INGRID: Yes I understand... but he said many times the same thing... every year he says the same thing. And when he was in his previous job, I always believed him...

How else can Tom get a business up and running?

INGRID: Of course, he has to work.

Hold on, we've got the beginnings of an understanding... he has to work but you [Tom] may be prepared to stop an hour earlier at weekends, an hour earlier on Saturday and Sunday. Two hours a week isn't the end of the world... That sends a message to Ingrid and Dan that they are very important to you.

TOM: You have to understand the boss I work for...

So how is he going to know?

TOM: Well, he's got cameras and he phones...

Say to him, "Look I'm very good at my job... I also have a family." When do you normally leave at weekends?

TOM: Five o'clock Saturday, four o'clock Sunday.

Five and four o' clock – so why not leave at four and three?

TOM: They are the hours I've agreed with him.

Okay, well go in an hour earlier on a Saturday and Sunday. Then at three you've still got time to do something with Sue and Dan.

TOM: That's something I should do.

Ingrid, how do you respond to that?

INGRID: I don't know. Normally, he...

Never mind about normally, how do you respond to that now?

INGRID: He's not going to go anywhere – go for a drive or whatever.

That's very negative.

INGRID: I don't know. He never drives me anywhere. I don't want to go alone somewhere...

TOM: Don't give me that. How can you say that? You must have been to every coastal resort in the south of England, you have.

INGRID: I haven't...

TOM: You have... Name a place where I haven't taken you. I mean, how can you say I don't drive you anywhere?

You're being defensive again – who do you both have to provoke?

INGRID: I just don't believe you. For instance, last Saturday, I said, "I'll pay for dinner, let's go for dinner..." He texted me, "I prefer to be alone." I thought, "Okay he wants to go with his friends." Then he rang me back and said, "Okay let's go" and I knew that he...

TOM: *(interrupts)* That's not true. I didn't want to go out. I

229

didn't want to go anywhere. I don't want to hear you saying that...

Don't get angry.

TOM: *(getting cross)* That's completely not what I said to you. She said I wanted to be with my friends. I did not say that...

Hold on Tom. She didn't say you said you want to be with your friends. She said she *thought* you wanted to be with your friends... that's not the same thing.

TOM: Okay, yes.

INGRID: He wanted to be alone... he wanted to go to the pub and see his friends.

TOM: No, no, no.

Okay, let's take this apart. You text Tom at work and said let's go for dinner. Tom, you said what?

TOM: I can't remember exactly. I hadn't slept for a few days. Sleeping has been quite bad and I felt so shattered, I didn't feel like going out for dinner. I just wanted to be alone.

What does that mean: "I just wanted to be alone"?

TOM: Really, Greta Garbo, that's what I mean.

But where?

INGRID: In the pub...

TOM: No, I just wanted to come home and be on my own. I'd driven up and down the motorway three times that week. Each time I had so much on my mind mentally, I was going through so many things.

Okay, but then you changed your mind...?

TOM: I thought if I don't do it, it's going to look bad. She's going to assume. So we went, we had quite a nice meal. Ingrid paid for a nice dinner.

The point is he did say yes...

INGRID: Yes he did... I didn't enjoy it anyway. Because I begged him to go...

TOM: You didn't beg me.

The way you're talking now, you're not going to get the best out of it....

INGRID: okay. I'll tell you from my point of view...

You can in a minute, but what I'm saying is, it's possible that working at the rate he's working, he will be tired. Fine. Then he says "I will go for dinner. He said he had a nice time... so you say, "I didn't enjoy it."

INGRID: I felt that he didn't want to come in the first place because so many times he said no, he couldn't say no any more.

So how can he please you?

INGRID: I don't know. He can but over the last couple of months he's been out three times a week,

TOM: No, no, no.

Let Ingrid say her bit.

INGRID: I just felt, "Why would he want to go out all the time?" I'm fed up staying here, cooking. I want to see other people as well. I just go to the park with Dan, blah blah blah. It's so routine. Then Tom says "I'm so knackered, I don't want to go anywhere... but he has been out three times.

Can I just ask you both something? Most couples go out together. Everyone has their own life as well but they also have a life together and...

INGRID: I know.

TOM: We're doing that. With regards to the dinner thing,

231

Ingrid's probably asked me to go for dinner a couple of times in seven years – don't look at me like that, Ingrid. She bought dinner and that's the first time I can remember it happening ever.

So that's a good thing.

TOM: Yeah.

INGRID: It's not true... It's not true. I pay all the household things, toiletries, this furniture...

TOM: Did I not take you and Dan to Sunday dinner three times last month?

INGRID: I have been paying for many years myself.

TOM: Ingrid, did you, me and Dan go for Sunday dinner three times last month?

Hold on, I'm wondering why you're buying so many meals out anyway?

TOM: Sunday dinner – it's nice to have Sunday dinner together.

Do you see how you're talking to each other? You're each trying to prove to the other person, the other person is "bad". Gillian and Penny are saying over and over gain, don't worry about the behaviour of the other person, concentrate on what *you* do and why you're doing it. He says "I've taken you out for lunch three times", and you're winding Ingrid up as well by saying...

TOM: I'm correcting actually...

You said it must be the first time in seven years that she's paid. The point is that you're still jabbing at each other, you're sparring all the time.

TOM: I get defensive. I have every right to correct something,

Yvonne, that's just not true. I don't want to be confrontational but if I hear something that's blatantly untrue...

INGRID: I did take you to dinner. We just speak such a different language – I don't know what it is. In the last two weeks [Ingrid had been off work, ill] I was reading books about relationships.

Psychology books?

INGRID: Yes, yes. My point is that Tom is 36 and his mum is still washing his shirts. She washes his shirts so he can go out like his father. There's no responsibility for him at all – just go. That's not going to happen any more. I told his mum, "I really appreciate your help but from now on Tom is going to wash his own shirts. He's 36." She said, "No man in England washes his own shirts..."

TOM: I would suggest that's my mum's sense of humour, Ingrid. She was being ironic. *(To Yvonne)* That's just gone straight over her head...

INGRID: His mum is domineering a lot in this family – she came to our washing basket and was taking out clothes, and I said don't do this. This is terrible. She's trying to help but...

Are you saying it's important because she feels she has less authority in this house now?

INGRID: Yes, I don't know – maybe she sees it's very stressful and she's trying to help... *(unclear: Ingrid talks very fast and is upset)* I was really thinking I was going to leave, three weeks ago... I thought "He doesn't want to be here so why are we together?"

TOM: It doesn't mean that I don't want to spend the rest of the time with the family but I need some time to myself... I want to be with Dan and Ingrid but in the right environment

So Ingrid, you were going to leave but then you changed your mind?

INGRID: It's all been so miserable, I thought, "Why am I doing this?" I'm forty – I'm going through something in my head.... maybe a mid-life crisis. Is this what I want from life? Is this man the right one for me? We hurt each other all the time But if I take Dan he would probably suffer. How could I take him to another country? Our problem is that we don't have time together – we are both pressured. We haven't had a holiday together the two of us, ever.

How do you feel, Tom, when Ingrid says that?

TOM: Yeah, we do need time...

INGRID: That's why I always say we haven't led a normal life. The reality Tom is that you want to go out with your mates. I'm in the house. That's the reality for years. How can I expect anything to change?

Ingrid, that was then...you can't keep saying...

INGRID: But he's still behaving the same way. His father has done it... it's in his genes...

You're undermining the chance of change because you're predicting failure and if you predict failure, failure happens. You're constantly talking about Tom's behaviour but actually it's your own behaviour you need to look at. Then, one day, he may bring you flowers not because it's Mother's Day but because he wants to – and you won't mind even if they are the wrong colour. We are talking tonight about more positive change – so where is the positive change? It may be that you end up splitting up – I don't know – but, at some point,

expressing anger has to matter less than seeing the sense in both moving forward.

INGRID: I have to change, obviously.

But if you keep saying it's not going to happen, it's not going to happen...

INGRID: It will happen, but Tom, you know how fucking knackered I am.

TOM: Yes.

INGRID: I'm doing all the household work... just before you came, Tom did the washing up for the first time this week...

TOM: Second time...

INGRID: I'd be happy if he did a little more of the household things. Friends would say, fucking hell! Why don't you leave this man...

TOM: Do you know something Yvonne, Ingrid letting off anger is why we're not progressing. I think we need to get away from all this, Ingrid. *(Ingrid interrupts)* Ingrid can I speak? If you want a place to go away and scream in or an effigy of me to beat up, that's fine – but can we use this to be constructive?

INGRID: *(talks over Tom)* You have to change yourself as well...

TOM: If you don't want to see something positive, we may as well go back to what it was before... We don't want a forum for you to be angry. It's not helping Ingrid, do you understand? This isn't moving us forward.

If you are concerned about this anger, maybe the answer is anger management.

INGRID: I'm not angry like that.

TOM: I never get angry with anyone.

INGRID: Sorry, your brother, your father... I take responsibility for some of the things I say. I take responsibility for pushing you in the face, I take responsibility but you have a temper...

TOM: *(sarcastically)* Oh, you have a temper, *(laughs)* thank you, Ingrid, thank you.

What's the issue here? You're now arguing about who has the worst temper – are we agreed you both have a temper?

(Tom and Ingrid laugh)

TOM: Yes, we both have a temper.

INGRID: When I was thinking before you came, shall I tidy this house because it was like a bomb had hit it, I was thinking if you came here you would see the problem. Then the vacuum cleaner broke and it was making funny noises, the place was an unbelievable mess.

But you didn't do more cleaning... That's very, very impressive...

INGRID: No, only because the vacuum-cleaner broke.

(All three laugh)

There, you're laughing now.

INGRID: We laugh often, it's just when you come here, then we say everything...

Maybe I should just stop coming and let you get on with it... What did you think about the last report? The low self-esteem stuff?

TOM: I think, yes. I've had depression for as long as I can remember. I just have degrees of it at any one time. I don't necessarily think it will ever go. It's not a slur on Ingrid. It's nothing to do with her – it was there before you.

INGRID: That's right. You admit it.

TOM: Of course I do, I'm happy to say that...

INGRID: You never admit it...your confidence...

TOM: It's nothing to do with confidence Ingrid, please. I am confident. Depression wears you out –I find it hard to turn off. My mind's always racing. I'm always thinking. I'm quite obsessive when I'm thinking about things. Problems... solutions. It could be anything, it's something in my character....

Are you on anti-depressants now?

TOM: No, they put me on stronger ones. And the strong ones I felt totally not myself so I stopped taking them.

What Ingrid said then, you said that he hadn't admitted...

INGRID: He's never said to me, "I'm so insecure".

TOM: It's not insecurity, Ingrid. It's not insecurity... What do you mean by that...? I'm not insecure. It's depression.

INGRID: Low self-esteem...

TOM: Possibly, in some respects. I suppose because our sex life is down the pan it's got to effect me. I must have low self-esteem in how I see myself.

You're both working very hard; you have very little time together and you're both exhausted – so it perhaps isn't surprising about your sex life?

TOM: Sometimes, with depression, you get incredibly lethargic, really, really tired, not normal tired. You just want to sleep for a week... I've learned to live with it. It's with me all the time. It doesn't bother me. I'm not worried about it – I just get on with it. I'm never going to do anything silly, obviously...

Tom, you're living with depression and you're not worried

about it. Why not do something about it?

INGRID: He went to the doctor with headaches, the pain was so bad.

TOM: To be honest they've really cleared up, neuralgia headaches, but one time... I can tell you, I'm under total pressure and it doesn't help, Ingrid, when you say things to me like, "This isn't going to work." You've been saying that to me for the past six years, since I first started to think about launching the business. "This isn't going to work... it's just a dream."

INGRID: I haven't.

TOM: You have, but never mind, listen...

(Ingrid and Tom talk over each other)

INGRID: You don't tell me your dreams.

TOM: The trouble with you is that you don't see the dream. I'm making something happen...

What did Ingrid just say to you?

TOM: She said you had to make the dream or something

No, she said you don't tell her your dreams.

TOM: I've just told you what I've been trying to plan for I don't know how long....

INGRID: We are not included in your business Tom, me and Dan...

Is what you're both talking about intimacy – or the lack of it? Sex is about intimacy, talking about each other's dreams is about intimacy...

TOM: Talking about intimacy, forget sex for a moment. We're so far away from sex it's unbelievable and Ingrid knows if we're on our own for half an hour, we argue. Sex is something

238

you do when you have a normal relationship. We never kiss, we never hug, we never say nice things to each other...

INGRID: I was the person who went as a child to hug people, I've begged you to hug me...

TOM: Tell me what sex and intimacy is. Sex starts from intimacy, which starts from kissing and hugging. You don't hear what I'm saying at all.

Hold on...

INGRID: We went to a pub, and you came there and you wanted to show everybody, "This is my wife..." He tried to kiss me – go away! I don't want that kind of behaviour.

TOM: I came to the pub and...

Let Ingrid finish Tom...

INGRID: You behaved like an animal. He came to me and kissed and hugged me like this *(in a very high voice, mimics Tom)*. Go away! I want a man to kiss me like a man. I like kissing but you have to say "Look at us!" I can't stand it...

TOM: Ingrid, there's only a certain number of excuses you can make. I'm the one trying to kiss you every night and you're the one who offers the cheek. We went out a couple of weeks ago...

INGRID: One month ago

TOM: Ingrid said she'd meet me. I came to the pub hoping it was going to be the start of something, "Kiss me, for God's sake, kiss me..." because she won't kiss in public so it's a big thing.

INGRID: You wanted to do it in front of everybody.

What you're both talking about isn't about "to kiss or not to kiss" – it's because most of that is rooted in intimacy and a

sense of peace with each other. It's obviously easier to show affection when you're not angry with each other and maybe that will take a little bit more time.I don't think you can order up the kind of lover you want. You can't say I want you to kiss like this.

TOM: I'm the best kisser in the world anyway, aren't I?

(Ingrid laughs)

TOM: You said I was the best kisser, yes you did... The whole point is I just wanted to give you a kiss in a way that anyone would give you a kiss. Not in a certain way.

Basically, showing affection in public is a bit of a thing for Ingrid, she's saying.

TOM: I'm too full on.

What she's presumably asking for is a quieter demonstration of affection and then you might get away with it in public – there has been a common ground somewhere between you, hasn't there?

TOM: I think, if you're going to kiss me, just kiss me. If I have to plan a kiss, Ingrid... The day I have to plan a kiss...

INGRID: Everyone was looking at us because we were in the middle of the pub.

TOM: No one was looking at us. The pub was full, there was nowhere to sit, so why feel the spotlight was on you? I just walked up to you and kissed you...

Now, you're arguing about...

TOM: *(laughs)* ..About who kissed who. Ingrid, I think this is the most ridiculous argument we've   had.

It's not an argument. It's about a bigger issue of intimacy and how you demonstrate affection to each other. Instead of

240

looking at your own reaction to intimacy and sex, you're looking at the other person and saying, "You're not doing it right." Both of you, you're always looking for disappointment in each other.

TOM: Hold on, why should I be presented with someone's cheek, when I want to kiss them?

Gillian and Penny say some people fall in love with a person whom they think is a better version of themselves. They think they've met someone special and gradually they realise they are just an ordinary person...

(Ingrid laughs)

You're not sure about that?

(Tom and Ingrid both laugh)

TOM: Ingrid's looking at me and thinking, "What the hell am I doing with this man?"

INGRID: When I came here [to Britain], the person I saw had disappeared...

He hasn't disappeared, he was never there anyway. Love is about illusion as well as other elements too.

TOM: The novelty wears off.

And gradually you begin to see the other person as they are – and that's when you have do the hard work if you want to stay together.

INGRID: I don't think Tom is ever going to leave me.

But what's the point of staying if you're going to be miserable?

INGRID: My father left me when I was a child. I always think Tom was quite strong, he was pushing me to the limit, asking me to come here.

TOM: I never gave up.

INGRID: I just felt *(shrugs)* "okay, I'll come."

We have to stop now but both of you are behaving incredibly constructively – certainly more than the last time.

TOM: But it was good you saw the real thing.

CHAPTER TWENTY-THREE

June – Gillian and Penny's sixth report

At the beginning of the process Gillian and Penny had warned not to accept at face value the picture Tom and Ingrid painted of each other. Initially, to me, Ingrid seemed more afraid of intimacy than Tom not least because of her father "abandoning" her twice (moving out of the family home, and then dying young). Now, I wasn't sure.

Tom kept his life in boxes, as Gillian and Penny had pointed out. As long as the boxes remained self-contained, he could maintain the illusion of being a successful business-man, a dutiful son and an involved father while still living the life of a bachelor – going out when he chose, working long hours, and keeping Ingrid at a distance. What I wanted to discuss with Gillian and Penny was how Ingrid and Tom could be encouraged to develop more of a life in common, and what might that mean for Tom's "boxes" and the issue of intimacy?

***

Tom and Ingrid show signs of becoming more reflective. Still, Ingrid appears desperate to have her voice heard and doesn't know how to make Tom or anybody else hear what she has to say. She's very provocative because negative attention is better than no attention. So she provokes Tom. She sees a huge risk in being hopeful because she'll be disappointed or may have to experience a great loss... and loss has been a recurring pattern in the relationship so far. Tom appears to have a need to control. At times, he patronises Ingrid and puts her down. He allies himself with Yvonne and uses her words to scold Ingrid and get her back in line. Perhaps he doesn't realise how often this is a pattern? Tom washing his own shirts is a positive step. He is setting boundaries, he's drawing back into his life as part of a couple. The danger is that he can then say to Ingrid, "I did what you asked me to, what more do you want?" He ought to try and avoid framing this change as if he's done it for Ingrid – he's doing it for himself as well.

Tom is pretty certain that Ingrid is dependent on him. She often says Tom won't leave but Ernest Jones, Freud's follower, had a notice pinned near the couch where his patients lay, "Always think of the opposite". Ingrid wants to be claimed and cherished by Tom – that's human. He may be standing in for her fantasy about a father who makes the little daddy's girl feel special. She wants a lot from him that she didn't have when she was young. The expectation on Tom is quite heavy, and perhaps he doesn't have the confidence to meet those expectations. Does Tom sometimes set himself up to fail? Perhaps Tom believes he has tried his hardest to meet Ingrid's expectations but he is already judged as failing – and in that apparent failure is a fear of loss of control? Tom might ask why control matters so much to him.

They still have very poor communication – but there are strong signs of improvement. They are both frightened that the other person won't hear what they are saying, so they exaggerate. They frequently use absolute words, such as "never". They spend so much time protesting and defending. What they don't use much is "because". Instead of saying "I feel bad because..." they say, "I feel bad and it's your fault".

Regarding Tom's work, Ingrid can only repeat her scepticism. What they can't seem to do together is to look at Tom's fears, his worries about failure and rejection. Ingrid has predicted his failure so often he may believe that he can't afford to be honest and show his vulnerability, which adds to his pressure.

When Ingrid invited Tom to dinner and he expressed his desire to be alone it was a profound rejection of Ingrid. Tom didn't want to acknowledge that. If the reason for not going was tiredness, why not say so?

They are beginning to have a positive dialogue – Ingrid, for instance, talks about their lack of time as a couple and Tom agrees. Another good moment is when Tom acknowledges his depression. It is very positive that he is being so reflective. Ingrid reframes what he says and says it's insecurity which labels him and backs him into a corner. Then she tries again with low self-esteem and he's okay with that, so

Ingrid is trying to find a common language that they can both accept.

Ingrid and Tom are also beginning to have a very important discussion about sex and intimacy. They both know when they discuss it, what it's really about. Tom is taking what is traditionally the female role. He associates sex with kissing and hugging but as long as they are both so angry that's a turn off (although anger can sometimes lead to good sex). Ingrid appears very conscious about being 40. Perhaps Tom, who is five years younger, finds it difficult to put himself in her place on this issue and understand her sense of vulnerability – what she calls her "mid-life crisis".

They each talk about their dreams. Dreams are particularly important for both of them because their reality often tends to be disappointing. They might need to think about why they have the dreams they do. Is Tom's to become a successful entrepreneur? What does Ingrid want – a baby, a big house, a big car? This is where she needs to use the word "because". Another baby because... a big house because...? More security, more status or something else? Ingrid does have dreams – she is very open about her understandable need to have something to look forward to, something to give meaning to the routine of life. Perhaps if they shared the dreams of what Tom's work could mean for them as a family, and Tom could recognise that Ingrid is asking for a gesture of recognition about her need to be attended to, and to matter to him, they might then have some shared hopes and a common dream.

Both Ingrid and Tom have very punitive figures inside

themselves. Tom believes he will be "got" if he makes the wrong move. In turn, Ingrid is unconsciously very punishing of Tom and herself. She puts herself in the wrong a great deal, she sets herself up to be criticised. They've got to become more conscious of this pattern – if they recognise the pattern, they can change it.

They both need to shift a bit – if they do, they may find themselves in a better place but they may also risk the marriage. If they fail to shift they will continue in the miserable format, either with each other or with a different partner. Ingrid and Tom might reflect on the following remarks they made and what they say about themselves. For example, Tom said, "She's looking at me and thinking, 'What the hell am I doing with this man?'" And Ingrid: "We speak a different language... You don't tell me your dreams... Why would I believe you?"

Towards the end of the meeting, a dance of intimacy was taking place. Tom perhaps fears intimacy because it might swallow him up. Ingrid yearns for it but her negativism, self-punishment and past experience in the relationship means she doesn't believe she will ever achieve it.

Still, there is a sense of something more constructive emerging.

CHAPTER TWENTY-FOUR

...and they lived miserably ever after?

We were more than halfway through the project. If change was happening, it was at a pace that would see Ingrid and Tom octogenarians before the relationship was reasonably repaired. A marriage "revived" but only just in time for their death rattles. The mystery was why a couple would want to continue to live together so unhappily? If a genuine shift in both their attitudes wasn't possible, why not split up? I was also concerned that my involvement might have exacerbated their problems rather than helped. Sub-conciously, were they reluctant to relinquish the pattern of blaming because they now had an audience?

I'd also expected Tom and Ingrid, at some point, to form a united front and tell us to mind our own business. With a few months still to go, I read an article from the *New York Times*, headlined "Troubled Marriage? Beware of Therapy". The writer, Susan Gilbert, had taken a brief look at how efforts to save long-term relationships have evolved in the last few years. One experimental approach, called "integrative behavioural couples therapy"(IBCT) had particularly good results.

Traditional counselling techniques teach couples how to avoid or solve arguments by delving into the past. The integrative aim is to make the rows less hurtful by helping partners to accept their differences and negotiate a life in common – using tools similar to those employed in cognitive behaviour therapy. It makes how we live together more important than a minute examination of our childhood, to discover why we live together in the way that we do. According to Gilbert, two years after ending traditional counselling, 25 per cent of American couples are worse off than when they started, and after four years up to 38 per cent are divorced. Part of the reason for this poor success rate is that the quality of counselling and therapy varies hugely. In addition, many couples don' seek help early enough, when the partnership develops the equivalent of a couple of flat tyres. As John F Kennedy allegedly once said, (while ignoring his own advice), "The best time to repair the roof is when the sun is shining."

All the couples who opted for IBCT were judged at high risk of divorce and many were also "couples' therapy failures". In spite of that history, two out of three couples said their relationships had "significantly improved" for two years after going through the IBCT practical workshops (a longer term follow up has yet to be completed). IBCT appeared not unlike the help that had evolved out of the monthly meetings with Gillian and Penny. Perhaps, for Ingrid and Tom the experiment might yet prove more positive than negative. Nevertheless, my doubts remained. Might they be the kind of couple who stay together unhappily for life rather than make a genuine attempt to change?

American psychologists Joanne Davila and Thomas N Bradbury, in a paper published in the *Journal of Family Psychology* in 2001, explain that even in the era of the "easy" divorce, there are still some individuals compelled to live a lifetime in stable but profoundly unhappy unions. What Davila and Bradbury attempted to establish is what makes these partners stick so miserably together?

The easy answer is that miserable people find other miserable people to share their lives. Except that neither Ingrid nor Tom are "natural" downers – they just happen to make each other unhappy quite a lot of the time they are together. Davila and Bradbury looked at 172 newly married couples over a four year period. A complex set of assessment points weeded out unhappy couples who might shun divorce for religious, cultural, social or economic reasons, as well as those who stayed together "for the sake of the children". What remained were a number of couples whom, almost from the first weeks of marriage, were disappointed and discordant – yet they stuck it out. Among the reasons why, Davila and Bradbury say, is that these people give out "distorted attachment signals". They are individuals who are overly dependent, have low self-worth, show a fear of abandonment and may have an aversion to intimacy. Depression is also often an issue. Fear of being unworthy means they believe no else will have them, so they stay. Attachment insecurity means that these people are excessively focussed on the relationship and are constantly monitoring the other partner. They are driven to maintain the relationship at all costs, no matter how unsatisfying because their dependency needs are being satisfied in an unhealthy way.

Significantly, spouses who remained in unhappy marriages over four years had the highest level of insecurity from the outset – within the first six months of marriage. "This suggests that such anxieties do not develop slowly over time but are present practically from the beginning of and perhaps prior to the marriage," the authors pointed out. This group constantly showed even lower levels of marital satisfaction than the couples who went on to divorce. They also showed far higher levels of depressive symptoms than the divorced spouses.

The divorce-resistent couples also had poor communication and gave each other inadequate support, paradoxically increasing the very sense of dependency that keeps the miserably married together. Davila and Bradbury argue that this is a unique group – different from couples who develop a battle ground over time. This group is in trouble from the outset. They need to be identified and helped early.

In both America and Britain, there is little investment in the kind of early intervention that may help people to develop a healthier partnership. In the early months of wedded or cohabiting "bliss", however doleful in practice, what might make a couple accept constructive advice or develop the insight to recognise their own symptoms, and thus avoid being permanently chained in a matrimonial dungeon?

CHAPTER TWENTY-FIVE

July: Seventh meeting – Tom and Ingrid

This meeting was a surprise. Ingrid appeared much less angry but also more regretful of the gap between the life she wanted and the relationship she had. It was also as if she was beginning to articulate a new standard for herself and Tom in the marriage. If before she had thought herself "deserving" of bad treatment that included Tom disappearing all night, now she was beginning to lay down her own rules. She was also much more ambivalent about whether she could continue without real change in the marriage. Perhaps Ingrid's new thinking might encourage Tom to reassess what he risked losing? Or prompt him to disclose his own doubts about the future of their marriage.

Tell me about the shirts.

INGRID: Nothing has changed, nothing has really changed.

Well, there is one change because Tom's mother isn't washing his shirts.

INGRID: The issue isn't who washes Tom's shirts – his mum is still there wash, wash, wash... busy, busy, busy. I know she's trying to help us but in the end, he still hasn't learned how to look after himself, he still sees it as "women's work".

TOM: Women's work? What a load of rubbish. I don't think Ingrid likes my mum. I'm happy to wash my own stuff but by the time I get home, Ingrid already has the washing machine on.

TOM: I've washed up more and only been out half as much – once in the last two weeks.

INGRID: He lies on the sofa until one o'clock in the morning then you are so angry if me and Dan wake you up accidentally in the morning.

(*Discussion about the lack of synchronicity in their evening routine – Ingrid goes to bed early and gets herself and Dan up. Tom goes to sleep late and gets up in time to take Dan to school.*)

TOM: In the last three months we've had two big rows but it's been easily the best spell for years. Ingrid wants a quick fix and focuses all the time on the relationship not being perfect instead of trying to improve what we've got.

INGRID: Are you coming back [from work] an hour earlier? No. Every morning, you are knackered.

TOM: Every morning you and Dan wake me up at six am. You are loud, Ingrid, you are very loud in the morning.

(*Tom says they went out recently and were holding hands "half the night" – which is a positive step forward. Ingrid says how little they go out together and that evening was a month ago, on her birthday.*)

Do you think Tom is capable of becoming the man you think

you want him to be, Ingrid?

INGRID: He's in the process of understanding we're not in his parents' marriage – he is starting to grow up but it's difficult to forget the years when he was working nights.

TOM: That's finished and done, Ingrid. Ten sessions on and you're still going back to that – you don't want to enjoy your life Ingrid, I do.

INGRID: I do. Fucking hell! I phoned his dad and talked about Tom not doing enough and he said he would talk to Tom but he never did.

TOM: You phoned my mum at midnight when you were drunk. Ingrid has a mindset. She wants a quick fix. As far as I'm concerned, the curve is going up. The issue is to try not to constantly knock it because it's not perfect yet.

INGRID: I'm not 100 per cent sure I want to be here [in the marriage].

TOM: She's always implied that – the reason she doesn't kiss me in public is because deep down Ingrid, you think I'm not the right person for you.

INGRID: I don't know. I don't know what I want any more. I'd like to have a baby for Dan's sake – maybe for myself. To get out of the rat race, because I'm 40... I don't know.

TOM: You want a baby but not necessarily with me. Our marriage is very rocky and you're saying you want a baby. Mend our marriage first and then have a baby.

INGRID: My boss knows me better than Tom and work mates know me differently from Tom. He doesn't treat me seriously.

TOM: You try to be inflammatory about my family and that's

254

designed to hit a particular spot... You're angry with me so when you talk about my parents, you're really saying something about me.

INGRID: You've said so many times that you can't live in my country in a negative way that's ignorant and impolite. I want to go back. Sometimes I think I'm totally different when I'm back home. This country changes me.

TOM: I'd never generalise and say I hate an entire country. It's a practical issue of how I'd earn a living.

INGRID: We are "numb" with each other. We don't have anything to guess because we already know the answers.

TOM: Since we've stopped drinking, it's got a lot better. Absolutely everything is to do with that. It's brilliant positive stuff for me.

(They debate about the role of alcohol in their relationship – with Tom, as always, saying it plays a significant role and Ingrid, as always, denying it.)

INGRID: Tom doesn't talk to me enough. He doesn't share his worries.

TOM: When I do share things, you use them as ammunition. The truth is if you're not happy with me. Don't piss around for the next two years and then go. I have to point it out to Ingrid that we are arguing less and I have tried to improve.

INGRID: But, we're not enjoying life... not as a couple, not as a family. Tom would be happier if he got into a normal sleeping cycle, not staying up until the early hours, and if he did more exercise. He doesn't do anything with Dan, they used to go cycling.

(*Ingrid discusses how she dislikes the way Tom looks now. She says he has put on weight, doesn't bother with his appearance when he's in the house.*)

TOM: I should do more exercise.

INGRID: I want more energy, not this kind of life.

TOM: I'm burning with nervous energy at work. I'm on the point of receiving a payment from the first sale of a house. The boss has said I can keep the profit from the tenth house that I sell but Ingrid doesn't want to hear any of this. It means nothing to her.

INGRID: I do want to hear, that's not true at all. You try and try at work, I know that, but then all you do is moan in the morning.

TOM: All I ask you to do in the morning is not to scream.

(*Tom says Ingrid is taking positive change and spinning it negatively. Ingrid says it's true, she's not crying so much but she and Tom have been living separate lives for so long.*)

What would you like to see happen, Tom?

TOM: I'd like a happy family with no worry about debts and bills and a nice school for Dan and a house with a garden.

INGRID: It's the first time I've heard that.

TOM: I've been saying it for two years... that's why I suggested that we move to St Albans where we could get something we could afford but Ingrid didn't want to do that.

***

The following day, Tom sent an e-mail – part of which read,

Ingrid and I had a bit of a laugh at ourselves after you went and I feel a lot better about things now than during the meeting, which was more hostile than I'd hoped for from Ingrid, in my opinion. However, inch by inch, we seem to be making slow and steady progress in many areas and I am grateful to everyone involved for putting forward the difficult questions that are hard to confront and helping us to see ourselves in a different light.

***

Gillian and Penny were on holiday in August, so Ingrid and Tom and I agreed to meet again in September. Tom continued to work, while Ingrid and Dan went to Scandinavia for a fortnight.

CHAPTER TWENTY-SIX
Crises

O n her return from holiday, Ingrid e-mailed me an
article from a web site which, she said, "describes my
feelings and our situation very well. So things could be better
here..." The article, "Why Women Leave Men" by counsellor
Willard F Harley Jr, was from an American web site called
"Marriage Builders". It began with quotes from anonymous
women, among them, "He lives his life as if he weren't married; he rarely considers me"; "We are like ships passing in the
night, he goes his way, I go mine..."; "I hurt all the time
because I feel alone and abandoned" and "The only time he
pays attention to me is when he wants sex..."

Willard argues that women believe their marital problems
are created by husbands who do little or nothing to solve
them. Wives see themselves as a major force in mending the
marriage, so when they give up, the relationships is over. In
his experience, Willard says, husbands believe the expectations of their wives have grown completely out of reach. The

men feel they've made a huge effort to be caring and sensitive; they are under enormous pressure to increase their salaries and improve the way they treat their wives and children. Yet, in return they receive only criticism. "Very few men, these days, feel they have learned to become the husbands that their wives have wanted". Many give up trying.

Willard goes on to argue that it isn't more effort that's required from men but "a change in the priority of effort" to counter their wives' alleged feelings of neglect. A man's life is like the rooms of a house; one is allocated to his job, another for golf, another for his children, and one for wife. As he says, what frustrates women is that they are relegated to only one facet of a man's life when they wish to be integrated into it entirely.

Willard, as a counsellor, suggests that husbands adopt "a policy of joint agreement" and involve their partners in every decision they make. His advice to husbands is: "Never do anything without an enthusiastic agreement between you and your spouse". In that way, he says, a man learns to think about his wife's reactions. "The aim is to become united in purpose and spirit, not to overpower or control each other."

Couples in tune have already learned how to behave in sensitive and caring ways to each other, Willard says. Emotionally distant couples have more difficulty because they have become so accustomed to doing as they please, they are not aware of the chasm that exists between them. Follow the policy of joint agreement for even one day, Willlard promises, and a change will begin to occur. Wives' frustration is reduced and husbands and wives are each gradually "encouraged by the other's thoughtfulness". Men who meet their wives' most important emotional needs also learn to overcome their own selfish habits in the process and are rewarded by responses that are no longer critical, cold and dismissive.

Willard's theory has obvious resonance with how Ingrid sees her marriage to Tom and describes a very traditional male-female scenario. But, given the change, for instance, in women's lives, it's also possible to imagine the opposite scenario: a man shut out, peering through the windows of his partner's multi-room life. She makes all the major decisions, allocates a couple of hours a week to relationship maintenance and takes holidays with her girlfriends. Instead of believing he comes first, the man is convinced – even before the children arrive – he is last in his partner's priorities. She can't understand why he seeks more; he can't fathom why she wants so little of a life together.

American anthropologist, Helen Fisher writes in *Anatomy of Love, A Natural History of Adultery, Monogamy and Divorce*, "Baby boomers are travelling though society like a pig moving through a python, visibly changing our culture as they grow older." While the male mid-life crisis has been constantly charted, female baby-boomers, born in the post-war period may be the first generation of women to experience a personal epiphany in their fifties. For some female baby-boomers, once the children are raised and, after years of being a wife and mother, a "good" separation or an agreement to lead parallel lives, can appear especially enticing – they can be financially independent, they are free of domestic duties, their own person. Sex also plays a part. People in their mid-fifties are children of the 1960s. Many women in mid-life enjoy sex more. They no longer collapse into crimplene and cocoa as previous generations were expected to to. They don't have the anxiety of becoming pregnant; many are more secure in themselves and have long thrown off the shackles of their mothers' conditioning that nice girls don't. If they do not have a fulfilling relationship in which sex plays an active part, a reassessment can lead to radical change. Data from the Office of National Statistics shows that the number of divorces in the 50-plus age groups has trebled in the past decade.

But divorce isn't the only solution. In an interview in 2006, the American actress Kathleen Turner, aged 51, talked about how her marriage of 21 years to Jay Weiss had worked. The couple are now semi-detached: six months apart, six months together. "I've reached a turning point in my life," she said. "I'm part of that first generation of women who have done their child rearing... and now just want to go out there and explore. That's so exciting but I don't think Jay feels the same way. He's brilliant, attractive, intelligent; he's just a terrific man. We're not going to divorce. After all this time together I couldn't even think of being with another man. People ask what the secret of us staying together for so long is, and I always say, 'tolerance'. Things change so much in a marriage from the original reason you marry a person to the person themselves – you have to be flexible."

Pamela Stephenson, psychologist and biographer of her husband, comedian and actor, Billy Connolly, is also in her fifties. She, too, has taken "time out" from her marriage. She and her youngest daughter sailed 19,000 nautical miles across the South Seas. "It would be very neat and cosy if couples went through developmental changes at the same time. Sadly, it doesn't happen like that," she said in an interview. "Apologies for using a shrinky word, but the key to a successful marriage is to individuate. You need to be able to understand your partner's developmental needs and recognise your own. Go forward, have the experiences you want to have – and argue for them."

She added: "Giving another person permission to do what they need to do is tough. But those marriages that are good are the ones where one partner says, 'I do understand,' or even, 'I don't understand,' or 'This is extremely fucking threatening to me,' but gives their blessing."

Creating a relationship that makes both people relatively happy over the years doesn't have to mean living in each other's pockets. It can allow for each person to change at different times and at a different pace. It may mean time and experiences apart, as well as together – but none of that is possible if the couple's conduct towards each other constantly undermines. A review of a number of studies of what gives relationships "legs" comes up with a predictable cocktail: love, trust, respect, willingness to compromise, shared values, a balance between togetherness and independence, resolution of conflict, reciprocity and fairness, physical and psychological intimacy – and lots of small gestures of appreciation which incrementally signal "I cherish you" – without the words needing to be said.

CHAPTER TWENTY-SEVEN
September – Tom and Ingrid's eighth and final meeting

Before we met, Tom, Ingrid and I agreed to re-read all the transcripts and reports, the better to reflect back on the year. As part of that process, I drew up a list of the constantly recurring and sometimes contradictory negative and (less frequent) positive remarks that each had made about the other.

INGRID ON TOM

1. Doesn't do enough in the house
2. Believes childcare and domesticity is "women's work"
3. Too involved with his parents
4. Works too much
5. Prefers to see his friends rather than spend time with the family
6. Doesn't look after his appearance, health or diet
7. Doesn't "speak" my language
8. Wants me to be "submissive" like his mother – and

independent like his sister

8. Opted out of the family when Dan was a baby by working nights

9. At times, makes me feel excluded, stupid and "bad"

10. Blames our problems on my alleged drinking – alcohol is a symptom of what's wrong between us, not a cause

11. Withholds sex

12. Maybe having an affair?

13. Doesn't talk about his emotions

14. Won't address his depression or low self-esteem

15. Immature

16. We have no interests in common

Positive aspects

1. A "good" man

2. Very involved with Dan

3. Good sense of humour

4. Ambitious

5. Optimistic

6. Straightforward

7. Generous

8. Faithful

TOM ON INGRID

1. Shouts in public and private

2. Drinks too much

3. Doesn't show affection and cold

4. Fails to acknowledge that I work long hours to pay the bills

5. Obsessive perfectionist who never praises me so feel I can

never do anything right

6. Resents my parents

7. Nags Dan

8. Constant mood swings

9. Hypersensitive

10. Insecure, so texts and phones me all day

11. Childlike

12. Repressed

13. Expects to be paid for...

Positive aspects

1. Open

2. Honest

3. Good sense of humour

4. Speaks her mind

5. Unique

***

This meeting is to look through all the material and then for Penny and Gillian to give a kind of overview – do you think it's been a complete waste of time?

INGRID and TOM: No, no, no, no.

TOM: I think it's really helped me to think about how I've been in some ways. Sometimes you lose your grip on a certain reality – it's helped me to look at how I've been. Before I was always looking at Ingrid's behaviour. I'm aware now that I was not behaving as I should have been.

INGRID: Yes, he was a boy for so long.

TOM: As for helping our relationship, that's a difficult subject.

Why do you think that?

TOM: Because one will help the other – once things are out, things can happen, and we can progress. That's been the most useful thing, having someone who has an honest and objective opinion about how you are *(to Ingrid)* and how I was running away a lot.

You think you were?

TOM: Definitely.

INGRID: If he can admit he's done wrong but I always think he's playing a game – you haven't often said you've done wrong. He always says don't look at those first years.

But, if you've spent seven years living one way, it's not going to change overnight.

TOM: Ingrid, it's easy for me to admit I've done things wrong – I look back at the notes and see how I was. But why I reacted like that, that's your side of the notes for you to think about.

INGRID: All that running away. I can't believe that somebody can act in that way. I couldn't ever do that.

You're two different people and the chemistry will work differently for each of you – how you react to each other will depend on all sorts of things, your background, whatever. Ingrid, are you saying that this process has been a waste of time for you?

INGRID: Definitely not, no – I've looked back and really thought about what Gillian and and Penny have said.

In what practical way has it made a difference in how you feel about each other?

INGRID: In some ways, things haven't changed. We still don't

266

speak to each other like this when you're not here. Tom has gone out so much this year but maybe you do come home earlier. Maybe we're just so different. I don't know. When my relatives were here it made me think, because my cousin was like me... I don't know.

Do you mean you were like her when you were younger? What did you realise?

INGRID: *(upset)* Nothing, nothing. God, I'll tell you later...

TOM: It could be worse, it could be half-time...

What do you mean: that Ingrid is upset because she is having her period?

TOM: *(laughs)* I get from her "period", "half a period", "quarter time", "full time"...

INGRID: *(laughs)* Oh stop it...

This is a mystery to me. You have all the negative stuff between you and anger, but still there's a lot of laughter and humour, almost at the same time. So where does the laughter come from?

TOM: You've got to laugh. I've always thought it very important. Ingrid says it's self defence. I can see why. Humour is much more than just making jokes. It's a way of surviving. It's also a way of rationalising. If you've learnt to laugh at something, you've conquered something in a way.

I can understand what you're saying, Tom – but Ingrid, has the past year helped you to stay or go?

INGRID: I'm not going to leave now.

You say you're not going to leave but two sessions ago you were saying you might.

INGRID: I have to be realistic. How can I say to Dan, "We're going to leave now?" How can we live in Scandinavia? I can't go anywhere anyway.

Gillian and Penny might say that sometimes we tell ourselves these things to justify being stuck. As long as you keep saying, "I don't know whether to stay or go", there's no incentive to work on making things better.

INGRID: I'm not always like that —when I'm angry my feelings change.

So how are you going to build a more peaceful existence together? Or maybe you don't want one? Maybe it suits both of you.

TOM: No, this year has been so much better than last year for arguing.

INGRID: The reality today is that it's still hard, he's working all the time. We've been married seven years and we still don't know how we'd behave together if we had a normal life. I think, "What if he hadn't worked so much" – it would have been so much better – we're always struggling.

You're saying the relationship has never had its fair chance?

TOM: It would be good to see what would happen if we didn't have to struggle... I'm in another business so we're out of the frying pan and into the fire. Albeit for different reasons. It would be nice if we had a place and it had a garden and you didn't have to work so many hours. I'm just saying it would be nice to see what things would be like.

Sometimes people create a certain life for themselves in order to avoid their emotional problems.

TOM: I don't think that applies to me in this case. I'm not doing this for love.

Well, there's got to be some adrenaline in it.

TOM: It's my baby, isn't it? I can remember thinking about this idea back in 1977 so of course I've got an emotional attachment, otherwise I would never have got this far.

But do you see an end to the long hours?

TOM: Yes, next year definitely, no Sundays and taking holidays. In January I'm going to sit down with Ingrid and clear that up.

INGRID: Working bank holidays doesn't do you any good – it uses up all your energy. Nobody works then. What use is it? It's so stupid.

TOM: It's not that Ingrid.

INGRID: You're hiding behind your desk.

TOM: I understand Ingrid's point of view but from my point of view it's like an irresistible force and an immovable object, working for my boss.

INGRID: Even so, I want you to change... *(Both talk over each other)* But let's see what happens next year.

TOM: Ingrid, I've told you ten times we're going to have a holiday next year. Of course, we can't carry on like this but you've got to change, too. Your voice is so angry. It's really hard to talk to you when your voice is like that.

INGRID: It's never going to happen.

(Both talk over each other, angry)

I guess what Tom is saying is that he's said things in the past and they haven't happened, but it's different now. Ingrid. Can you give him the benefit of the doubt?

INGRID: Okay, okay.

TOM: It's just words. Ingrid say it as if you mean it. You never give me the benefit of the doubt ever, so do it. You're just nodding.

No Tom, Ingrid earlier gave you a commitment. She said, "Let's see what happens next year."

TOM: But she's still throwing things at me about this year. You said about me working bank holidays but you know.

No Tom. She's saying you're working all the hours because it's partly an emotional thing. Perhaps there's some truth in that, you've become attracted to somebody, your boss, who allows you to work and and who demands all the hours. At some point, it may be that you have to decide between your work and your relationship?

TOM: At the same time, my boss said after we sold another house that he had enormous plans...

But do enormous plans mean you working like this forever?

INGRID: That's right.

Okay. You've got the issue of long hours but how do you feel about your own behaviour in the relationship, Ingrid?

INGRID: I have looked at myself more. I hate myself screaming and shouting. But, you know, I cried often because I'm knackered. One day I'll wake up, say "Bye bye, fuck you." I'm not a fucking robot, I'm a human being. I'm scared. I don't say what I'm thinking – it's bad...

It's bad because you're not saying what you're feeling?

INGRID: *(upset)*

I'm sorry you're upset. It's very difficult.

INGRID: I don't try any more.

Some people might say as long as you say, "I'm going, I'm not going" you won't really have to do anything. Do you know

what I mean? It's a kind of power game in a way... Tom is always on probation. He never knows whether you're going or staying... In a way, each one of you is making yourself powerless as Gillian and Penny pointed out. Tom is working all the time so he has no power to influence the relationship and you don't know whether to stay or go so you've got no leeway to improve your side of the relationship.

INGRID: I don't know what to do.

TOM: *(angry)* I can move out, Ingrid.

INGRID: What?

TOM: I can move out.

INGRID: Yes, I think you're wanting to do that. Yes you can move out... fucking hell, you can go. He's playing games. Once he's got money, he'll say, "Don't think I'm staying here because I don't love you. Bye bye."

TOM: If that was true, we wouldn't be doing this would we? **Ingrid, are you perhaps doing what you did at the beginning? Predicting your own abandonment? You have got a choice. Tom can't win if he says "Okay, you're unhappy I'll move out" then you say, "I always knew you'd do this..."**

(Tom and Ingrid talk over each other)

Why do you two want to be unhappy together?

INGRID: Because we're bloody cowards.

TOM: I don't want to split up, moving out is a last resort but if we're at the last resort, we're at the last resort. I think our relationship deserves every opportunity and chances are, things are going to get worse before they get better.

INGRID: You started working as soon as I came here, but you're saying it's all about my dad.

TOM: I'm not saying that.

Can I just interrupt a minute, do you know how many times you've each said the same things to each other in the past twelve months?

INGRID: *(smiling)* I know it's unbelievable.

TOM: Ingrid can't move on.

But Tom it's both of you. You've got the perfect excuse not to invest emotionally in this. You keep saying it's your job. If your relationship is on the line. ou make a choice at some point, you really do. The other aspect you haven't talked about at all and it's the most important factor of all – is Dan.

TOM: Well, that's why we're here... to make a stable home for Dan.

INGRID: If I'm not happy and I'm his mum...

TOM: So what do you want me to do about it? What's your perfect answer?

INGRID: Be responsible for your family... Don't do everything for your boss.

Hang on, if you think this through rationally, you've got debts...

INGRID: That's right, more and more.

Is debt a problem?

(Ingrid upset)

TOM: My pay has gone...

INGRID: You earn more than me, what do you mean?

TOM: I didn't have a chance to speak, Ingrid. I didn't have a chance to open my mouth.

INGRID: I admit that sometimes I buy something. It's retail therapy. I don't get anything from him so I go to a shop but, if I buy even a pair of socks, I feel guilty...

Do you feel you buy a lot?

INGRID: Yeah...

TOM: I think we had 20 coats at the last count. *(smiles)*

INGRID: Every time I got to Scandinavia the Visa bills go up and then I'm struggling again to pay them off for a couple of months. It's the same thing all the time.

TOM: My salary... *(Ingrid interrupts)* Can I speak Ingrid?

INGRID: Okay, okay.

TOM: My salary has gone from £26,000 to £30,000, then £35,000 and it goes to £40,000 in January. I know it's long-term and then we can manage the debts and pay it off...

Have you got a lot of debt?

TOM: I've got cards and things, yeah... We've got a loan of £10,000 but there's only £4,000 left on that... Ingrid wanted to get another flat for another £200 rent per month. It's just ridiculous at this time.

(to Ingrid) **Why do you want to move into a bigger flat?**

INGRID: I want somewhere for my friends, my family to stay.

TOM: You've been sending me pictures of homes you want to buy.

INGRID: I'm just saying, let's go and have a look.

TOM: I will when it's more relevant.

(Ingrid and Tom talk over each other)

Ingrid, you want Tom to work less but you're e-mailing him houses which will require more money?

TOM: £275,000.

That's a very mixed message isn't it?

INGRID: Yes, it is.

So what's it about then?

TOM: The housing market has been down this year – that house won't be any more expensive next year. With my salary and your salary we can afford approximately £280,000. I'm predicting that we'll be able to buy at that amount.

INGRID: I don't get anything of what you're saying.

TOM: Basically, you're sending me houses that we could buy with our salary next year. In other words, Ingrid, do you want me to give up work? You're telling me to achieve what I've set out to do. You're supporting me...

INGRID: Of course, I'm supporting you...

What he's saying Ingrid is that the long hours are an issue. However, it pays for the house that you may have together next year – does that help [you to accept] that for now he's working long hours?

INGRID: Okay, before, when he worked in his last bloody job I really hated that place. He was always escaping.

(Ingrid and Tom argue over each other loudly about the hours worked in the night shift etc)

If you're going to try and improve the relationship, some of that is going to have to be put to one side isn't it? Okay, this evening you're giving Tom a telling-off because of the hours he works – rightly because they don't allow you to have time together. But, at the same time, he's giving out the message, "keep going because we can have a better life next year". Do you think you might have to do a bit of a trade-off for the next few months?

TOM: Perhaps a career is my way of saving this relationship? Perhaps that's all wrong but I know you want a house.

274

One of the things that came out in the interviews was low self-esteem but is it that you think you chose a man who isn't as good as you think you deserve?

INGRID: Maybe...

TOM: Oh yes, definitely.

INGRID: I think so, yes. In my own country, I thought I came from quite a good family. But my parents are divorced so at the same time I thought maybe I'm not good enough... I did, yes I did. Now I know nobody's family is perfect. Now I think how fucking stupid I was...

TOM: I want to save this relationship.

You're both so focused on what you haven't got in your relationship, you don't appreciate what you have got. Ingrid, Tom just made a huge pledge to you, he said he wanted to save the relationship.

INGRID: I do as well.

TOM: Sometimes I don't know why, I really don't know why.

INGRID: If I say this, Tom isn't going to like it but... I don't like you sometimes because you don't look after yourself.

TOM: I understand that, that's fine.

INGRID: You say I'm not going to wash myself or whatever. I hate that; I really do hate that...

TOM: You hate everything Ingrid.

That's not fair Tom.

TOM: These little things add up until every thing's a little thing.

You know where this perhaps comes down to? It might come down to depression. If Tom's not looking after himself?

TOM: I must admit I've been extremely low. The last time we

met it was Okay but the time before that was very, very, very low. She's been out of control. Out of control.

INGRID: What do you mean out of control? When I've been drunk or something?

TOM: You tell me, Ingrid.

Do you mean you've been having physical fights again?

INGRID and TOM: No, no, no.

INGRID: I went out alone three weeks ago. I came back and I was quite drunk. I wanted to go out alone. I felt good in a way, even though I came home really drunk.

You went out with a girl friend?

INGRID: No, alone...

TOM: She went out about nine o' clock and then fell through the door at... *(laughing)*

(Ingrid interrupts)

TOM: She came home at midnight.

INGRID: Not even late.

TOM: She couldn't stand up... fell over... broke the table.

(Ingrid laughs)

TOM: No, Ingrid, you were totally paralytic in two and a half hours... You couldn't speak.

INGRID: I remember exactly what happened.

TOM: The broken table?

INGRID: Yes, yes.

TOM: The way you came in two hours after you went out. You said you'd had a couple of wines and what else. This is the conversation we had – another whisky and another two drinks. Alcohol now is becoming too much.

INGRID: No, it's not Tom.

TOM: Yes, it is.

INGRID: It's not true.

TOM: I poured three bottles of whiskey and spirits down the sink. Do you remember when I had to do that?

INGRID: God, Tom that was a stupid thing to do. I was so fucking angry with you, that's why I went out. I am so fucking unhappy.

TOM: We're all unhappy Ingrid. Okay? You said "let's go out" a couple of times, and what happened? What happened three times in a week?

INGRID: You tell me what happened? We went to the cinema. *(Both shout at each other.)*

The key here isn't whether Ingrid got drunk or didn't. There's also perhaps another underlying reason why she is drinking or not drinking, and why you're concerned about her lack of control. And it's not obvious. It's distressing, isn't it, because it's also often an indication of someone's unhappiness?

INGRID: I would say.

TOM: You change so dramatically.

Most people do, though, don't they?

TOM: Not like this.

INGRID: I don't do it with my friends, only with you. Often on a Saturday, he can't share a bottle of wine with me. He can share alcohol with his friends but not with me. Oh God *(distressed)*. He said to me, "Let's go for a drink together after the cinema"... I wanted to go for a meal...

TOM: No. I said I'd drive you to the restaurant.

INGRID: No, you said you wanted to go home.

TOM: *(angry)* Did I say that? Did I say I'd drive you to the restaurant? I was driving. I said, "Just get out of the car. You're screaming in my face and I'm driving. Get out of the car!"

Let's talk about this. Soon we won't be meeting any more. What will you do? You say you don't talk like this when I'm not here and clearly there's still a big step forward to be taken in the relationship. You don't want to descend to the point where you destroy each other, do you?

INGRID: That's right. Without you we wouldn't...

TOM: We wouldn't be here... You've brought us this far, you Gillian and Penny, just by making us a bit more reflective.

The aim is to create a happier life, not just to think more about how miserable you both are.

INGRID: That's right – if everything happens as Tom says with money, and, if the business goes well, then we really face reality. I think then he won't stay with me. He'll go. It's his personality as well. He wouldn't stay with me. Once he's got the money...

You might be wrong, Ingrid.

TOM: What about the other week? I said, "Let's meet in the pub." You just started on about my family and I left you in the pub.

INGRID: My mum said to me, "Why don't we invite Tom's parents to Scandinavia?"

TOM: My dad says every year to my mum, where would you like to go? Australia, Italy, Wales? So my dad said to my mum, you decide, you work hard, this is your holiday.

So what's wrong with asking if they want to go to Scandinavia?

TOM: Nothing, nothing at all. Ingrid, all I said to you was ask them, but my mother will ultimately decide...

278

What Ingrid seems to be saying is that you keep your family in a little cocoon, Tom.

TOM: I certainly don't want you screaming and shouting in front of them, or me or vice versa.

INGRID: On his mum's birthday, I said, "What about a present for your mum?" He's always saying to me, "Don't buy [her] anything".

TOM: You asked my mother what she wants for Christmas and what does she say? She'll say "Get me a little plant or something." True or not? What do you think? She wants something simple but you want to buy her big things...

(Both shout at each other)

What are you actually arguing about here – a pot plant? Isn't this symptomatic of something bigger, Tom? It's not about what you buy. Ingrid is saying that she feels she can't have a healthy, open relationship with your parents because you're more worried about them finding out what's going on [between you two] than...

TOM: I certainly don't want to upset them because there's no point in upsetting them...

Don't you think they know already?

TOM: Yes.

Ingrid is saying she wants to get closer to your family, not that she hates them.

TOM: But she only gives them one word answers... When my dad tries to talk to you about Scandinavia and he knows a bit about the history, you say, "That's right", "Yep" – one word answers. You know that's true Ingrid.

So why would you do that, Ingrid?

INGRID: Because, when I first came to this country, they didn't ask me much. I didn't understand the language at first but then he never asked me anything.

So you're blanking him?

INGRID: No, I didn't know what to say. He speaks cockney. I don't feel they ask much. Your mother speaks all the time but she doesn't ask anything.

Perhaps if they know there's trouble between you they'd rather not ask. That might be out of affection for you too, Ingrid, because they don't want to have to take sides.

INGRID: You protect them so much.

(Ingrid and Tom talk over each other)

Hang on a minute, Tom, are you protecting them for the right reasons?

TOM: What do you suggest I do? Make my mother upset and worried – because that's what's going to happen?

But they're upset now.

TOM: More so if they knew the depths of the problem, without a doubt. We've got into such a rut, love, why is it so easy by e-mail or on the phone but it's so bloody difficult at home?

INGRID: You're not interested in me sexually – it was clear even when I was pregnant.

TOM: You've pulled away from me for years. How can we have a sex life until our relationship is sorted out?

INGRID: If I'm honest, I don't like your fat belly. You don't think about yourself one bit and I don't like that. My dad died in his forties. He felt so stressed, he was busy, He didn't take his medicine as he should. He had no exercise and went to Lapland skiing and died. *(To Yvonne)* It's the first time Tom

280

has heard that. You're Dan's father, you can't do that...

(Ingrid goes on to discuss whether she wants a baby or not)

TOM: A baby means less money, less sleep at the wrong time in our lives and the relationship...

INGRID: I can't say what I think.

TOM: Say what you mean – just be straight.

(Yvonne interrupts) **Listen, if we hadn't done this for the past twelve months, do you think you would have been better or worse off?**

INGRID: I think we would be really, really unhappy and...

TOM: Just having a bloody good go at each other is a good thing. If you were a counsellor, it wouldn't have worked.

INGRID: I never used to talk about my past but then I realised I didn't have anything to hide. Fucking hell, it's good to be able to talk about the first few years, to get it out. Without this I don't know what would have happened. Maybe he would have gone forever. I know he loves me .

TOM: *(laughs)* "Deep down I want to leave..." *(said ironically).* She sends me kisses with e-mails, don't you? **What will you do next? We don't want to leave you stranded?**

INGRID: We would go to counselling. Definitely now I want to go to counselling...

TOM: Do you know what would be a good line of work? Someone you could sit down with, and just sound off... A professional listener. I hope this is the start of the end, if you know what I mean. I know it sounds a bit funny but maybe the start doesn't always come when you think it's going to come. I've got realistic expectations. If we can reflect enough and understand enough and forget the past, we can do it. We can move forward. We can do other things. When you sent the e-mail of that house, Ingrid, I saw it as a good sign. You're impatient as I am about these things...

INGRID: I am thinking ahead about the house.

TOM: I'm not going to piss off when I start making money, Ingrid. Look at me, I'm not going to do that. Let's be honest, you want the house because if I do piss off, you know you can keep it. So we're going to do it anyway.

Tom, what Ingrid wants you to say is "I love you, I want you to stay with me..." Not about buying the house.

INGRID: I don't want a big house or a big car. I didn't get married for money. I wanted to be with you, bloody hell!

TOM: *(laughs)* Don't sound bitter about it, Ingrid.

I think you've misunderstood each other. I think Ingrid is saying to you Tom that you see the worst of her because of the tensions and everything... Ingrid, you said at one point you didn't want a big house.

TOM: It's not about a big house, it's about a house of our own with our own garden for Dan. That's all I want. Every time I mention money, you like to think I'm obsessed with money...

INGRID: I don't want to be his mum. I want to be a normal wife with a normal husband, but you're not a normal husband. You are really difficult, you say yourself that you are a free spirit, a single man. I mean really...

TOM: When I said "free spirit", it's just a silly expression, it's just me saying... :"ook, I'll never be single again. You're Dan's mum and I'm Dan's dad, I'll never be single again. I want us to be together."

282

CHAPTER TWENTY-EIGHT

October: Gillian and Penny's eighth and final response

Meeting Gillian and Penny for final time, it was clear that happy ever after was a still a long haul awayBoth Ingrid and Tom were finally stripping away illusions about themselves and laying aside the false promise that it would all be better next month, next year, at the next deal. Could they rebuild the marriage on more authentic foundations? Would they want to?

***

Ingrid seems very frightened and unhappy – emotions that are emerging more clearly now that she has her anger under greater control. Her father dying young reinforces, on the one hand, the profound concern that Tom's lack of fitness may mean he "abandons" her because he falls ill and dies. On the other hand, she fears that he may also leave her if the business is a success because she is not "good enough" to stay with.

Women who lose their father at a young age find it very difficult not to feel responsible for failing to keep their father. Both Ingrid and Tom need each other but they are also fearful of needing each other so much. She over-values Tom, and then denigrates him. She talks about Tom a great deal. He is her focus. Ingrid still seems to find it difficult to talk about herself – perhaps she has yet to find out who she is because she allows so much to be coloured by Tom's judgements of her.

Tom is beginning to have a better knowledge of himself but he may overvalue work and success – not least because it also allows him to retreat from intimacy. They both find intimacy difficult and unconsciously between them have constructed a relationship that allows them to find different ways of avoiding it. Tom has his goal in work so he feels he is travelling somewhere – Ingrid feels more stranded.

She is reacting rather than initiating and laying down terms in the relationship. Perhaps she believes she can't risk saying what she really feels in case Tom does leave – so she acts out her frustration and sadness and unhappiness in her binge drinking, retail therapy and alleged "moodiness".

If you look at Ingrid's position from her perspective, the positive element is that she is not alone. But she appears lonely within the marriage. We repeat that both Tom and Ingrid are operating defensively, afraid of what might happen if they were to make themselves vulnerable and open up to the other. They might ask themselves – "what's the worst thing that could occur if we let down our guards?" They lack basic trust, so they can't be generous with each other –

and it's generosity that is one of the vital ingredients that helps to nourish a relationship. Possibly one of the reasons why Ingrid holds on to her grievances about the first seven years so steadfastly – apart from her justifiable sense of hurt – is because they fill her sense of emptiness. Even if she has little else, she has her grievances.

Perhaps she needs to address the reasons for this sense of emptiness. Ingrid is so over-preoccupied with what Tom is doing, she's neglectful of her own life. We have only glimpses of what she appears to want. Another baby? On the surface, of course, she may simply long for a child and/or believe her biological clock is against her. She has also said she would like Dan to have a sibling. Another baby may also be a route to intimacy with Tom. One or all these issues may feed into her longing for a child – a desire that appears to ebb and flow. But Ingrid also has a preoccupation, at times, with perfection – an illusionary goal often sought by those who lack a sense of self-worth.

Perhaps Ingrid desires a second chance to do something "well", even "perfectly", something which didn't go as smoothly as she'd hoped the first time – given the medical complications that followed Dan's birth and then Tom's absence. While understandable, Ingrid might consider whether that's sufficient reason to have another child – given that babies often add to tensions between a couple rather than alleviate them.

We don't know how Ingrid really feels about the role of alcohol in her life – other than she drinks because, she says, she is unhappy. The part of her that deals with the issue of drinking is also the part of her that too readily feels bad about herself, so there is a lot of denial. She understandably finds it difficult to discuss her alcohol intake without associating it with blame. This feeling is exacerbated, sometimes, by Tom's need to hold the moral high ground. Unconsciously, he may be exercising control over Ingrid by his ambivalence to her drinking. At times, he encourages her to drink – on other occasions, he chastises her.

Is Tom aware of how unhappy Ingrid may be – and how he emotionally blocks her out? Tom is now more physically present in the relationship – but a great deal of him is still locked away emotionally and out of Ingrid's reach. Crucially, the presence of a third person appears to have been a factor in Tom and Ingrid's relationship, from the outset – there's Ingrid, Tom and Tom's mother; then Ingrid, Tom and Dan; and Ingrid, Tom and Tom's boss. On each occasion, the third person indirectly and directly becomes drawn into the conflict between Ingrid and Tom – and also distracts from Tom and Ingrid's ability to operate as a couple.

The process of the last twelve months has created another triangle – Tom, Ingrid and Yvonne – but hopefully this time, it may prove more constructive. Now, Yvonne is part of their triangle, that frees Ingrid and gives her space. It may also have exacerbated her fear of the looseness of Tom's ties to her – but that "looseness" is a fear, not a fact. Tom is perhaps more dependent than either he or Ingrid realise.

It's also possible that Tom does have some negative or at least ambivalent feelings about his mother which is expressed via Ingrid. Individuals may choose partners who allow them to make a break from a parent that they themselves are otherwise incapable of making. So the partner provides an excuse to create a distance between parent and adult child. Tom may also unconsciously feel he is in competition with Ingrid for his mother's affection.

Generally, a relationship works because the individuals involved have made a conscious decision that the relationship works and choose to see it in a particular way. A mental adjustment can itself put a different "spin" on events and emotions. To use a cliché – is the glass half full or half empty?

It might also be useful for Tom and Ingrid to recap on the six stages of a relationship, referred to earlier, to assess the stage they have reached:

1. Romance
2. Reality
3. Power struggles
4. Finding oneself
5. Reconciliation (working it out)
6. Mutual respect and love

Tom and Ingrid appear to oscillate between the third and fourth stage. The power issue is about who is going to leave. Ingrid constantly threatens she will go back to Scandinavia, then retracts. Tom offers to leave as a reaction. Ingrid, in turn, then reacts to his offer and treats it as "proof" that Tom really doesn't want to be with her. This particular "dance"they have developed is central to their relationship, and they know it.

Being left is a big issue for Ingrid. How she handles it is part of reaching and managing the fourth stage, "finding one-self". Of course, being left may prove a major trauma – but it is not insurmountable. Perhaps, for Ingrid, the fear and anticipation are infinitely worse than the outcome, should it happen. Ingrid perhaps needs to try and unravel her emotions around this issue, since it locks her into an unhealthy position in the relationship.

Ingrid also sees not having sex as another form of rejection. Tom's response is that Ingrid has pulled away from him for years – they can't have a sex life until their relationship is more stable. Establishing this as a condition may also allow Tom to run away from intimacy again. For Ingrid, the lack of sex leaves her without hope – literally, unloved. Paradoxically, the same may also be true of Tom. He has built walls around himself that only he can begin to dismantle – and that, too, entails stripping away self-delusions and really "finding oneself".

Some couples can travel through the stages of a relationship instinctively. They have an understanding that even when the relationship is fraught, their joint belief in their long-term partnership and the memory of what they have built that is good together, will help to weather the bad times. Research tells us that the very experience of negotiating and surviving tensions, strains and periods of upheaval, actually enriches the quality of the marriage or cohabitation for long-term couples. Companionship grows deeper; the sex life may improve and renew its erotic charge, and life together as well as apart flourishes. For those who find it more difficult –

perhaps due to an unacknowledged ambivalence about being in a relationship in the first place – the rewards aren't considered worth the effort that is involved.

Ingrid and Tom are at the stage in which they are only just beginning to understand each other's differences and why and how they relate to each other. Once they see at least some of those differences as strengths, rather than constant sources of irritation, they may be able to form a mutually satisfying relationship to the benefit both of Dan and themselves. Or, if they are unable to make the next major shift, they may decide that separation is preferable to living together in fear, insecurity and animosity.

CHAPTER TWENTY-NINE: POST SCRIPT
Revival – or last rites?

A few weeks after our last meeting, the relationship suddenly appeared to lurch spectacularly off the rails. Gillian and Penny had both said this might happen as Ingrid and Tom realised that they were once more on their own. But could the crisis also provide the catalyst that would radically shift a couple who were still "stuck"?

I received a series of e-mails which explained what had happened. First, Tom wrote:

> Things have been rough for us at times since our last meeting. I think much of what has gone wrong has been made worse by my reaction to problems and how I see Ingrid behave toward me. I have felt at my lowest for ages and seriously considered going. Ingrid wanted me to go. Ingrid has also been down, more so than normal. I know her debts are spiralling as mine were doing before. I still want to see how things would be if we were not so time-consumed and debt

290

ridden, and I have been working on something for a few months which, if it works will solve all our money issues. All the main points to a very complex deal have been agreed so I am very hopeful I will come back with a "piece of paper" á la Neville chamberlain 1938, and then pray my figures and sums are correct.

I know our marriage should not be based on finances but how would we be with no excuses for our failure so far? I cannot write too much now but when I read the reports I can recall us sitting down and the words being spoken as if we are back in the room. I can also see how desperately we are trying to be heard. This just underlines both how important communication in a relationship is, as well as how badly we communicate at present..

***

Two weeks later, I received an e-mail from Ingrid in which it was clear Tom's tendency to keep his life in very separate boxes – parents, home, work, friends, pub – had been spectacularly curtailed. Part of the e-mail read:

I have done lots of thinking about us and this process etc. We have been doing surprisingly well, maybe I need to touch wood...! Though before this we did have quite a bad period, Tom went out a LOT and I was really cross with him. One Sunday 2 weeks ago he did not come home at all. Then he went straight to work at 2pm. When I found out I rang his mum as he was out with his dad the night before I asked if he was there??? I knew he was not but this way they got to know the situation as well... I also told her some truths about his behaviour. Tom received some feedback, from his parents. I said I am going to leave him (I know I have said this before but this time was different – mentally ready now!) IF he does not change his behaviour!!!

I was really serious, I still am!. I even spoke with my mum about this and divorce (for the first time) and we had a good chat. She is backing me with this anyway. Since then, I have seen some significant changes in Tom's behaviour... hopefully this time it will last!

The next day, Ingrid sent another e-mail:

I did not touch wood yesterday... So read what happened last night. It started when Tom went out. I was happy about it, no bad feelings at all. He seemed to be happy. And result: he did not come home at all, not even in the morning. I needed to call his mum to take Dan to school... Tom's mum was not pleased. I was quite open with her. I said that this behaviour is nothing new. It had lasted all these years and I am not taking this forever. She asked if we (Dan and me) are moving to Scandinavia? She looked not scared but furious. I tried to be normal when Dan woke up. Huh! Here we are again. Tom is sorry but it does not help much. [His] problems seem to be more deep than I thought.

Ingrid then sent me an e-mail that Tom had sent to her, with his permission:

Dear Ingrid,

I am sorry, I slept in the pub after a late drink and that was wrong.I feel like I don't want to go home when I go out lately and this is a problem that has been slowly getting worse over the last year. I know I can change this and also that there is no excuse, I am upset for you and Dan, and my mum is rightly furious. I will try to sort myself out and am sorry if I hurt you. Having said that I have done nothing to be guilty of apart from sleep somewhere other than home, so don't make it worse than it is. I have been so unhappy, and under so much pressure at work that I have gone to extremes with my own time and realise that. SORRY – not a robot not perfect not unfaithful not a bastard just drunk just unhappy

Tom

Ingrid later sent another e-mail in which, perhaps for the first time in the marriage, she laid down boundaries for Tom. "Poor you," she wrote, "I actually feel sorry for you but I do not think I want to share my life with you. I am not sorry for myself any more and I do not need you to make me feel bad... Good luck with your chosen route and have a nice time with Jim (Tom's 'pub' friend). You deserve each other....!"

A couple of weeks later, Tom went to Spain on a business trip. He had found his boss increasingly difficult to work with but believed he had little choice but to persevere. The trip proved successful, relieving some of the pressure. He also found himself doing something he had never done before – opening up to strangers in a bar. He met four ex-pats and spent the evening drinking in their company. He discussed his marriage and the experience of the previous twelve months. On his return, he e-mailed me to give me their advice: *Stay in the marriage and try harder.*

Tom said he was no longer sure how he felt about Ingrid.

***

Three months after our final meeting, and eighteen months after we first met, I went to see Ingrid and Tom at their home. The atmosphere was very different. Ingrid was much calmer, more relaxed, more self-possessed. Tom, too, looked much more at ease – even through the occasional spats that still broke out during the conversation.

Ingrid joked that, for the next seven years, she had a new argument with which to pursue Tom – the book. He no longer worked on Sundays. The two were considering moving to Scandinavia – although now Ingrid was less keen. Tom had yet to go for help with his depression. At one point, Tom said to Ingrid, "I want to learn to love you again."

I could be completely wrong but, even while bickering, they didn't look unhappy in each other's company. And that's a big step from two summers ago. They also – for the first time – talked about their relationship in the present. How they felt about it *now* – not how it might be next year or when the money came in or when they both worked fewer hours.

I asked Tom and Ingrid as well as Penny and Gillian to write about their view of the previous year:

INGRID:

Things are becoming clearer for both of us. It has helped enormously to be able to open up and discuss our relationship problems and we received lots of valuable feedback from Penny and Gillian. I have also poured out my emotions to people close to me and read lots of books related to this subject. All of which has helped me to know myself better. It's been a time of soul-searching.

This process has answered WHY both of us may have behaved in a certain way. It must have been difficult for Gillian and Penny to get to know us without seeing us, relying only on our comments and especially our constant blaming of each other. But perhaps that needed to happen, to live through those bad feelings again. In the end I think it cleared the air and it is finally turning into something positive. Provided that some significant changes happen, of course!

I see some issues differently from Tom and I don't always agree with Gillian and Penny but I don't blame them as some of Tom's comments about me were quite extravagant. For instance, I haven't been out that often with girlfriends – perhaps half a dozen times in the past year – nor do I drink as much as Tom implies. But I am not going to go through details and try to prove myself again. If Tom thinks that way, it is his feelings and I can't do anything about it.

Now I realise that there was still a little girl grieving/ missing the father she never got to know. I also see a link between my father and my husband and realise why I felt extremely bad about Tom's behaviour. I felt totally hopeless every time he went out because it triggered that feeling of abandonment. This is what I meant when I said, at the beginning of the process, that there is "Something about my past that I need to find out". I wasn't aware of this "grieving" before.

I certainly don't mean that Tom's behaviour has been acceptable and it's all down to how I feel about my father. Not at all! It's just taken me time to realise that he goes out not because of me but as a result of his own upbringing and emotions. I let him treat me this way and thought I deserved it! I feel very strongly now that my marriage has to change. I am not going to be miserable and waste my life.

I have probably taken too much responsibility in our relationship. Gillian and Penny were right – I have concentrated a lot on what Tom is doing (or NOT doing;) and put my own needs aside. I think both Tom and I placed ourselves in an emotional deep freeze to avoid getting hurt any further. I've been blind to the fact that it's not just me carrying emotional baggage but Tom as well. I hope this process has helped him to see behind not only his behaviour, but mine too.

Recently, the three of us had a wonderful family Sunday together, the best in a very long time – but when we came home, Tom announced he was going out for a drink. It's as if we become close – and then he runs away again. It worries me that, in his behaviour, he is also a role model for Dan...

Still, I see more hope than ever in our marriage, regardless of whether we end up together or apart. The most important result of this process is that I believe I have a RIGHT to feel happy in my life!

Tom:

Over the last year and more we have been confronted by our past and present and perhaps this has given us the ability to shape our future. From the outset, it was vital to me that there was enormous trust from us in Yvonne. I don't mean professional trust as in any form of counselling. I mean trust rooted in the conviction that someone genuinely wishes both to learn and to offer help not just to us, but to other couples who are also having a bad time. I saw that Yvonne had a passion for the subject and was not just "doing a job." The importance of this to me cannot be overstated.

Even though I don't agree with some observations made by Penny and Gillian, the whole point about the importance of the "earned trust " is that I have faith in their judgement.

It has been difficult to reconcile the person on the page as me sometimes. I have been going downhill for a long time and the relationship was rock bottom when the sessions started. Every time Ingrid and I tried to discuss difficulties, the discussion would break down into an emotional confrontation that just caused more problems. This process has forced us to confront ourselves and answer questions that we would prefer not to have been asked.

I have been going deeper into depression without even realising it. I have basically forgotten about speaking to Ingrid about my feelings. In fact, every form of communication or sharing has stopped let alone sexual intimacy.

I still don't know what the future will hold for Ingrid and me. I've kept many things to myself like the amount of personal debt I have mounting up as well as facing massive job insecurity, My boss for the past three months has had cash flow difficulties. I didn't tell Ingrid as it wasn't good news for Christmas. I was so worried it started to affect my sleep and general health.

I am now going to discuss these problems with Ingrid and work hard to find solutions. I am tied to this job and this boss because of the hard work I have invested. I don't want it to be for nothing.

It is important to me to have a career for myself and more importantly for my family. I think I have probably got to the point where I sometimes think everything depends on my job which I know is wrong.

I have said to Ingrid that we should move to Scandinavia and I'm ready to do that. I would like to leave something growing here, though, for us all to benefit from one day. Perhaps moving to Scandinavia is me saying to Ingrid, "What matters most is for us to be a happy family." I hope Penny and Gillian agree!!

I have always believed that Dan was the reason we should go to counselling. In my view now, this is a fallacy. Dan will surely only feel the benefits once we can restore a loving and happy home life.

Ingrid and I have to learn to love and trust each other again as we are both numb in our feelings toward each other. I think it has been a shock for both of us to see how we behave, through the eyes of others. I do not like the person in the book and I do not like what I have allowed myself to become. People need to have a trusted viewpoint to shake them from what they regard as "normal" behaviour.

There is a long way to go but, in some regards, we have also come a long way. I hope to make some progress with Ingrid in the coming months and to be less selfish in my attitude to the things she really cares about. I have to be more giving. I hope this will be the start of a new beginning although we may not realise that immediately.

I'm grateful that something very real and positive has emerged from this process.

GILLIAN WALTON:

I hope that this project might encourage other couples to have confidence in asking for help – of whatever kind suits them best. Vast numbers of people avoid seeking assistance because of fear or shame. Perhaps Ingrid and Tom's experience may allay some fears.

What attracted me to the process was also the possiblity that, as a team, we might offer something to Ingrid and Tom that would encourage them to be less defensive and more thoughtful; to encourage more understanding and compassion for each other. The opportunity to discuss issues with Yvonne and Penny was essential for this.

I went into the year with similar concerns to Penny about ethics, consent and confidentialiity. They were resolved as the relationship between the three of us developed organically, in a way that mirrored the relationship between Yvonne, Ingrid and Tom. What also helped was the fact that both Ingrid and Tom were aware that they had choices and that they were in control of the process.

I would like to applaud Ingrid and Tom for their courage

and for their capacity to be reflective despite their turmoil and distress. Their commitment to try to gain understanding for themselves and for the sake of their son is impressive. Exploration and understanding are essential before change can happen. Receiving undivided attention was probably the most therapeutic aspect of all.

PENNY MANSFIELD:

Whether the source is – poetry, prose, social science or literature – the evidence is clear: the "happy ever after" outcome of romantic love is a myth. A compelling myth – but a myth. The reality is that relationships are troublesome and, if they are to last, those troubles have to be endured – somehow. That "somehow" is endlessly fascinating.

Investigating it is the work my colleagues and I do at One Plus One. We have interviewed hundreds of men and women over the years about their relationships. In the complex, paradoxical world of partnerships, we have found that only those who create a common narrative enjoy the benefits of having someone who is "there for me " in the long-term.

Often, spouses become entrenched in their individual perspectives and find it hard to take account of what their nearest and dearest are saying, thinking, feeling – hoping for. Relationship counsellors aim to offer such couples the help they need to do this. But when marriages are in trouble, most couples shun such intervention.

Yvonne wanted to see whether one couple in trouble could be helped to help themselves by talking to her, an outsider who is not a counsellor – in order to also provide insights for others in relationship difficulties.

Her proposal to set up this experiment instantly appealed to me, but I was cautious too. One Plus One is always being approached by the media – TV especially – to help them take the lid off married life and lay bare personal relationships. Of course, other people's marriages are fascinating, but after interviewing so many couples I know they can also be very mundane. Yet the media shuns the mundane and wants to display the extraordinary, and this distorts our knowledge of relationships and titillates rather than informs.

I believe that understanding relationships – why they matter, how they work, why they go wrong and how to cope when they do – must be founded upon evidence. Through research, interpretation, understanding, we build knowledge – that knowledge strengthens families and society. For example it is especially important for parents to understand the impact of the quality of their own relationship on the relationship they create with their children.

My involvement in the experiment required Yvonne to:

> select the couple according to our objectives
> not take sides
> not place any child in the relationship at risk
> respect each spouse's perspective (not seek THE truth)
> cope with the process
> find a way to use me and Gillian to support her, especially when difficult issues arose.

How were the needs of the media going to mesh with

my concerns? Yvonne conducted the venture skilfully and with integrity. This experiment has been extraordinarily valuable. It confirmed many of the conclusions we have drawn from more than 30 years work at One Plus One but it helped me understand them in a new way. I am sure readers will find that Tom's and Ingrid's accounts mirror something in their own lives or the lives of their friends.

***

Over much of the twelve months, I wondered if either Ingrid or Tom, or both, might pull out – so painful were some of the meetings. It's a tribute to the commitment to try and do the best by their son, that they continued.

What struck me about Tom and Ingrid was that, no matter how unhappy they had become, both of them remained very wary of divorce. "Better off without him/her" has become almost a mantra of our times. Yet life post-divorce can be a hard terrain, shadowed by regret. Financially, women are often significantly worse off and men only marginally better off than their ex-wives. Emotionally, both pay a price.

Depending upon the circumstances of the marital breakdown, many women, in the short-term after separation, say they are relieved and liberated. They repair friendships and take up new interests. Inevitably, they are more content than they were when they were in the eye of the matrimonial storm. It is men who are more likely to suffer depression and became isolated, and their work may be affected. However, for both men and women, divorce can leave a scar that never fully heals.

In a study published in *Psychological Science* in 2005, psychologist Richard E Lucas analysed eighteen years of data involving over 30,000 German men and women who were asked to rate their life satisfaction on a scale of one to ten.

He discovered that a sense of happiness generally returns around five years after a divorce, but that it never returns to pre-divorce levels. The emotional landscape is complex. He also discovered that those who divorced appeared to have been less happy during the happiest years of their relationship than those who stayed married. However miserable the relationship, divorce isn't necessarily the only route to happiness – as Tom and Ingrid appear to realise.

Both have now said that they are considering counselling. Good-quality counselling can improve communication between a couple, reduce anger and make an individual more self-aware and intuitive about their partner's needs. It can also improve self-confidence and it may bring clarity of thought where before there was confusion. Sometimes, it allows couples to separate more amicably than they otherwise might have. Poor counselling, on the other hand, can make a bad situation worse. And counselling, of course, is not the only answer. It is one of many solutions.

In the past, members of an extended family often offered guidance. That may still happen, but we have yet to devise innovative ways of offering support at a time early enough to make a difference.

Good-quality relationships are the pulse of a society. They

affect all aspects of life – government, social care, the public purse, health, wealth, education, employment, crime, and the economy. Yet consumerism and the drive for ever-increasing profits dictate that we work harder and longer. How to fit everything in? Instinctively we know that what matters most is in our lives are the adults and children we treasure, the people who, through good and bad, we hope return our love.

We know that if we build a relationship that works, then the chances of our children and grandchildren achieving something even better is greatly enhanced. Nevertheless, many of us hold fast to an irrational conviction that the only preparation required for marriage is the piercing of Cupid's arrow. Love will do the rest. On the contrary. Those couples who regard themselves as reasonably content share a conviction that living happily ever after is an achievement not an automatic right.

In the case of Tom and Ingrid, their quarrels have shown a clear change. The repetition of grievances has significantly diminished. Self-reflection has begun to take the place of accusation and blame. The challenge ahead is whether they can forge a happy relationship based on optimism, not disappointment.

Research tells us that the very experience of negotiating tensions and strains and learning why certain pressure points inflame arguments can itself somehow add to the quality of a long-term relationship. In the process of trying to understand what the angry words really mean, two people may well discover that they are also fashioning a better way to express their love.